MEMORIES OF HARWOOD
in the early 1900s

JOHN BERNARD KETTLEWOOD

1905 - 1986

Edited by Mary Atkinson

Published 2005
by Voyager Publications

All rights reserved. No part of this publication may be reproduced, stored in a retrieval system, or transmitted in any form by any means, without prior written permission from the publisher.

ISBN 0 9525392 7 6

Printed by Bullivant & Son, York. Tel. 01904-623241

Cover photograph: Sherburn Street, Cawood, c1905

FOREWORD

BERNARD KETTLEWOOD

It is nearly twenty years since Bernard Kettlewood died in May 1986 at the age of 81 years. He was born in Cawood and lived there all his life. He and his wife Idona (Isy) who died in 1984, had no children of their own, but were dearly loved by all their family, and especially by the younger members who loved to hear stories about his childhood in old Cawood.

In the early 1970s, having recently retired into a new bungalow at the age of 65, perhaps it was the ideal time to look back on a life well-lived and to get his memories recorded on tape, as told to his great-niece and nephew, Diane and Paul, who were then seven or eight years old.

The first time I heard these tapes I felt they were priceless, and it seemed a pity not to get them transcribed so that others could enjoy them too, so with the permission of his family I decided to do so. I am indebted to Mike Race and Van Wilson of York Oral History Society and to Mary Owen for putting me in touch with them.

Thanks are also due to those who kindly loaned photographs with which to illustrate Bernard's memories; namely Michael Bell, Addie Hunt, Mac Jackson, Michael Johnstone, Kath Pullein, Kate Warrington, and of course, Bernard's family. Sincere thanks also to Mike Cowling for his help with photographic matters.

Profits from the sale of this booklet will be donated to the fabric fund of All Saints Church, Cawood, in memory of Bernard and Isy.

Mary Atkinson
2005

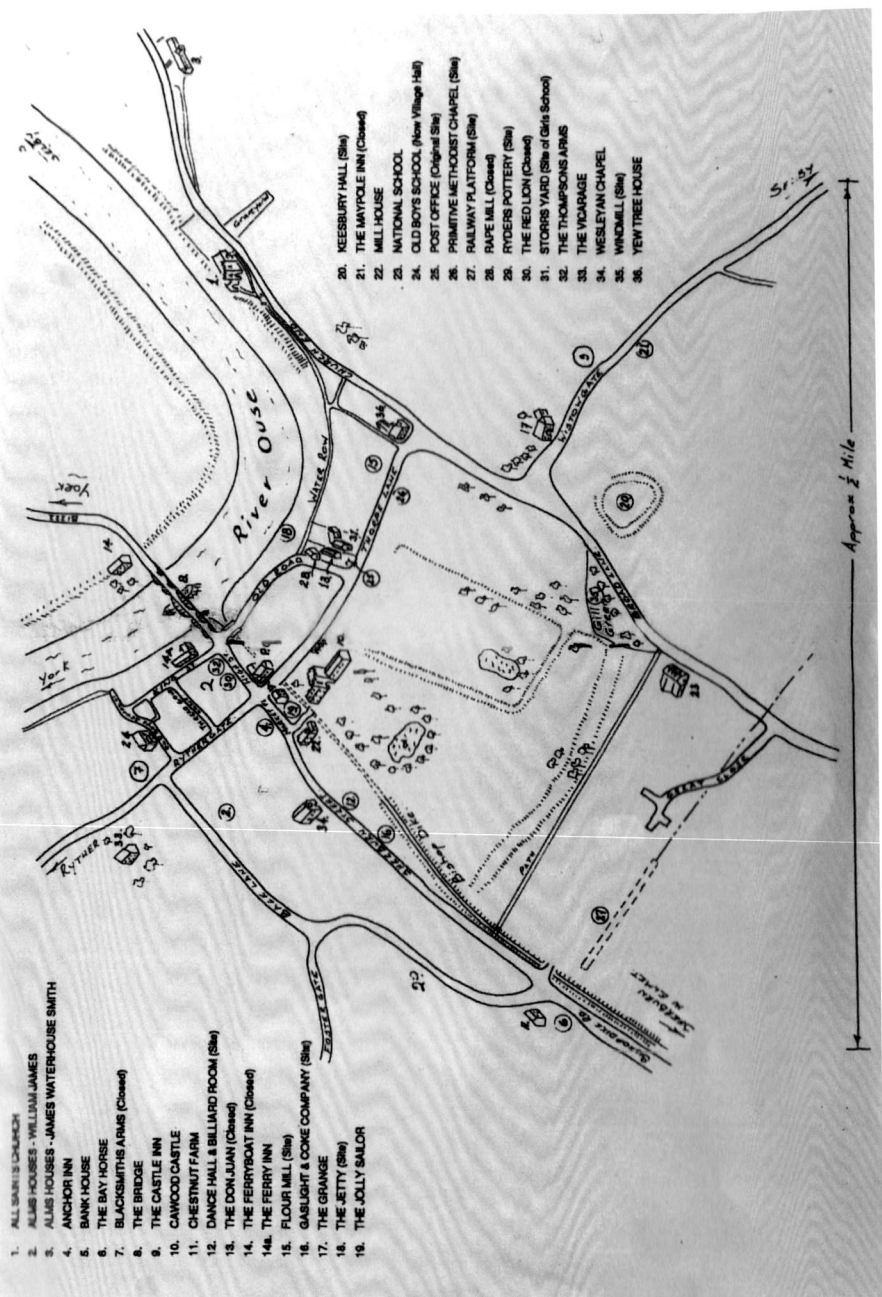

Village map as in Bernard's time.

INTRODUCTION

Bernard's reminiscences cover a wide range of changes in village life. He speaks of the time when Cawood had gaslight before electricity came; of having to pump water before piped water came and of the first cars in the village and the first bus service. Throughout the tapes one can hear Bernard's love of the village and especially of farming. His ability to remember and name so many fields must be almost unique today. He speaks of the old ways of hiring farm workers; of small houses and large families; of village football and cricket teams; of salmon fishing and pig-killing; of paddling in the Bishopdyke and skating on the fields in winter; of Cawood's Fair and Feast; of the large congregations at both church and chapel; of the respect expected and received by those in authority, clergy, schoolteachers and police. Altogether a nostalgic look back on what has helped to make Cawood the village it is today; a look back to life lived at a slower pace, but one in which the way was clearly signposted and which Bernard lets us see what he at any rate, definitely thought was the better way. Not for Bernard the fuss over expectant mothers and badly behaved children whose parents spoil them!

He tells of the time when Cawood had a working railway station, a working flour mill, important trade on the river and a crane on the foreshore, ten public houses, numerous small shops and a good supply of local tradesmen.

It may be of help to readers to pinpoint the present-day position of some of the places Bernard mentions. First of all the public houses of which only three remain; the Jolly Sailor in Market Place, the Castle Inn in Wistowgate and the Ferry Inn (sometimes known as the Commercial) in King Street. Six are in occupation as private dwellings. The Don Juan is now 4 Old Road, the Anchor is 4 Market Place, the Maypole is 14 Wistowgate, the Blacksmith's Arms is 18 Rythergate, the Thompson's Arms is 21 High Street and the Red Lion (later to be Mr Jim Todd's shop) is 7/9 High Street. The Bay Horse in Bishopdyke Road has been demolished to make way for housing.

The slipway in King Street disappeared when the floodwall was built. The Grand Hall used to stand between 21 and 23 Sherburn Street. It consisted of a billiard room on the ground floor and a ballroom with a beautiful dance floor, refreshment room, cloakroom and balcony upstairs. The chapel in the cemetery has long since disappeared, but the bell from the bell-tower can still be seen outside the flats in Chestnut Road. The old Boys' School is still *in situ*, owned by the Feoffees and leased by the Parish Council for the use of the village. Joss Middleton's Yard that Bernard speaks of is now 11 Sherburn Street and the 'gun man's' house is now 8 Sherburn Street. Wormwood Hill is still where it has always been, at the far end of Old Boys' School Lane. The flour mill stood where 21 & 23 Thorpe Lane now stand.

The railway station, of which Bernard seems to have been so fond, stood where Sylvan Close is now, at the far end of Sherburn Street and comprised offices, platforms and weighbridge. The railway line ended at Cawood and ran through what is now Great Close with a railway crossing in Broad Lane. The stationmaster's house is now 30 Broad Lane.

That part of Bishopdyke, which runs along High Street and part of Sherburn Street, has been piped in. No wading in the dyke for children of this generation! In any case, it would seem to have been a health hazard even in the days of ash-pits when some of the houses next to the dyke took the opportunity of 'direct' sewage disposal!

Old Road is part of the original road, which ran from Wistowgate down to the bridge. Nowadays it refers to that part from outside 3 Thorpe Lane to the bridge. The bridge was opened in 1872. It is quite surprising to note that for fifteen years, until the 'new' road was built in 1887 (from 18 Thorpe Lane to the crossroads in the centre of the village), all traffic to and from the bridge from the Wistowgate side of the village must have had to use the riverside road. The carriage entrance to the Castle was from Market Place until the 'new' road was built. This road cut the Castle garden in two, leaving part of the garden and the summerhouse on the far side of the road from the house.

According to the minutes of 'Cawood Town vestry meeting' of 8 July 1886, there was a notice from the Ecclesiastical Commissioners and Selby Dam Commissioners, announcing their intention 'to make a highway in the parish of Cawood commencing at a point opposite the P.O. in Wistowgate and leading over Bishopdyke into Sherburn Street'. The P.O. at that time was situated where the road now turns down to the river (i.e. Old Road), and Wistowgate being what we now know as Thorpe Lane. At the same time a public footpath known as the Castle Footpath which led from where present-day 16 and 18 Thorpe Lane stand, across the Castle farm stackyard, through the Castle gateway, in front of the Castle farm and out into Market Place, was stopped up. Village gossip at the time said that it was because the lady of the house did not take kindly to village people constantly passing in front of her house! It was, in any case, a big improvement.

From the family album: Bernard and Isy's wedding at All Saints Church, Cawood, in 1930.

Quite a few private houses, which were originally shops, retain their shop windows to this day. At what was Mr Parker's in High Street, the butcher's slab can still be seen. The druggist/chemist's shop is now a hairdresser's at 1-3 Rythergate. The old saddler's shop is the closed shop at 2 Market Place. John Wetherell & Son, grocers, later a café, later still a pottery, is now 8 Market Place. Bernard's parents' shop and bakery is now 12 Sherburn Street. Pilmer's is 38 Sherburn Street. John Smith's shop is 4 Sherburn Street. Bartle's shop, later Turner's Bridge Foot Stores, is now 18 and 20 High Street. Grundill's the butcher's shop, later Ella Neville's cake shop, is now 4 High Street. Lambert's shoe shop is now 8/10 High Street. When Bernard refers to the place where Jack Allison or Ray Goodrick lived, he is referring to where originally yard and farm outbuildings were situated, where 4 Rythergate now stands.

Paul Gibson and Diane Culkin, great nephew and niece, were the first recipients of Bernard's memories of old Cawood.

If Bernard were to see Cawood now he would have to admit that the condition of housing stock is much improved since his day and the apparent standard of living is higher. Certainly there are more cars! Whether or not he would prefer the Cawood of today is quite another matter.

CAWOOD

When I were a lad there were about three joiners and three bricklayers in Cawood. You could get a pair of boots made in the village; you could get a suit made in the village, and you'd some of the best tradesmen there were in the village. There were ten pubs, but in them days with all them pubs, they had to have a job. One old man at Thompson's Arms used to work at the Castle [Farm], but all the other pubs had a bit of land, and that's how they all made a living. They couldn't make a living out of the pub, same as today, they can't make a living out of it. There used to be, as I say, ten pubs . . . there used to be the Thompson's Arms in High Street again t'bridge, and t'Ferry House [sometimes called the Commercial], in King Street; there were the Anchor and Jolly Sailor in Market Place; there were t'Bay Horse up again the station and the Blacksmith's Arms in Rythergate; there were Don Juan in Old Road and there were the Maypole and Castle Inn in Wistowgate. [Also the Red Lion in High Street].

Odd characters

There used to be some rum old characters in Cawood. [Local pronunciation Cow-ud]. There used to be an old man lived down . . . well, his sisters had a shop in Rythergate, where the doctor has his surgery, new doctor [Dr Edwards, Posterngate]. They were milliners and they had a brother called Richard. They went to live up in the almshouses, [in Church End] and he lived in one house at the side of the passage, and his sisters lived in one at the other side. One sister was bedridden, and old Dick . . . every time he come into t'village in summertime, he would have a saw under his arm. I think he used to sharpen saws for folks and he used to have a broad bean swab on his ear, he'd summat matter with his ear, and he used to come down with this broad bean swab on his ear. Tommy Lund, little Tommy, used to clean up for him on a Saturday, and no wonder Tommy's a queer 'un with queer sayings because he's heard some!

There were one or two poor old folks lived in t'almshouses, they called 'em Waterson and she used to have an old man who used to wheel her in a bath chair. This old bath chair had wooden wheels and iron tyres on, and by! it took some pushin'. She used to have a walking stick with her, and if t'old man didn't do what were right, what she wanted, she used to hit him with t'stick. Well, one day she'd hitten him and he shoved her down t'bank at Water Row there and skelled [tipped] her out. They used to take her to Wetherell's I think on a Friday mornin' to pay her bill and order her groceries, and they used to take t'old chariot right up to the door. Well, she were getting out one day and she slipped and she got jammed in the

John Wetherell's shop in Market Place, Cawood, a branch of the main business which used to be on the corner of Finkle Street and Gowthorpe, Selby.

doorway. There's two doors, and she got jammed and ever after that when she come they used to open both doors, so she could get in. When she died, I know they made her old chariot into a cart for an old man called Tipney Elcock. He used to collect horse muck out of the streets and sweep up, and somebody made him this cart. It had two back wheels on the front and a swivel wheel on the back and then he used to go round t'streets with it. He were a rum old feller were old Tipney, he allus used to be getting drunk, and the bobby here were allus after him and he took him three times to Selby, to court, and the old magistrate says at t'finish: "Don't anybody else get drunk but Tom Elcock?"

You know where Johnny Buckle's house is, Willow House? [2 Old Road]. Well, that used to be a basket maker's place. Two brothers had it called Varley, and their dad didn't used to do any work when I were a lad. He always used to walk down the street with his walking stick across the back of his back, with his arms wrapped round it. These two brothers used to make baskets, tatie [potato] baskets and hampers with a lid on, what used to hold about six stone and then they used to send 'em away. These two always used

Cawood Bridge in the early 1900s, featuring from left: Herbert Wormald, Mr Maltby (a relation of Mrs Wormald and an annual visitor to Cawood Castle), Austin Booth, an unknown boy, Tom Booth the bridgemaster and Twig (dog).

to leave work together at ten minutes to twelve to go home for their dinners; one would go by Water Row and t'other would go by t'new road, they never walked home together. One on 'em used to say: "It's a dourly happy New Year" and "It's damp and dusty underfoot".

Then there were another little place at the end of Johnny's, they knocked it down to build yon houses of Storr's. There used to be a little man called Jimmy Laverack there, what made baskets for folks. When he wasn't making baskets he used to be the band cutter on the threshing machine. When they were shiftin' t'thresher in the streets, a band cutter used to have to lead any horse what were a bit frightened, because horses used to be frightened of 'em in them days. They didn't like steam engines, you know.

Cawood bridge and river
And of course there was the bridge and the river and there was more river traffic then. There was one man used to look after the bridge in them days called Tom Booth and he opened that bridge more times in one day than they do now in six months and he never had any telephone or owt and he used to sleep in t'lobby when the tide were comin' up, when it were time for tugs. These tugs used to come and they used to have about six or eight

barges on, big iron 'uns with about two hundred ton of wheat and stuff on for Leethams Mill at York. Then they'd have a wooden 'un or two behind loaded with coal. Arthur Green's dad used to have one and them lads had to go with him. I know once they hit t'bridge and it sunk again t'boatyard, did a barge full of coal – took 'em a bit to get it up.

By the time he got that bridge shut many a time there were another packet blowing for him to open it again. There used to be four tugs belonging York Corporation; they called one Lancelot and t'others Ebor, City and Sir Joseph Rymer, and then there were another one or two what belonged Woods, some folks who used to tug. I used to carry stuff on tugs as well, and they called 'em . . . what were it? . . . Rose, Arrow and Graphic I believe it was.

By! There was some traffic on that river then. He just used to get that bridge shut many a time and it were to open again, and there were only that one man there and to see him 'go away' opening the bridge, it were summat out of t'ordinary. About every two years, he used to get some men and they used to paint that bridge, it were a picture. They used to paint all the iron work white, and all the buttresses and that were tarred, and if ever a ship run into it and knocked a lump off, the following week there were somebody come from Selby with a barge to put it on. Oh, it was in good condition then!

Cawood Castle farm
There was the Castle, that were a grand farm. Wormalds had it and they used to employ half of the folks in Cawood. He [Charles Wormald] had three brothers: one called Henry, we used to call him Whitey; one called Percy, we used to call him Eggneck 'cos he had a big lump on his neck and another called Herbert and they just had to work like the other men. He'd eight or nine labourers and he'd a feller called Tommy Stronach who reckoned to be his handyman and when he used to send Tommy into t'cellar to fetch some beer, he used to make him keep whistling so's he knew he wasn't drinking it. He took Tommy to Leeds with him one day and at dinnertime they went to a hotel for their dinners and he took Tommy with him and he orders what he wants does Mr Wormald. Then he asks the waiter for a serviette. Tommy Stronach says: "Aye, and bring me one an' all, if he can eat one, I can". This here Percy Wormald used to get t'men to plough the pie bottoms up where tatie pies had been. When they cleared them, he used to plant 'em with sprouts and then when they were ready, he used to go out hawking them. He'd pull them into a bag and he'd a bairn's potty for to deal 'em out with, tuppence a time.

Cawood Castle farm and house seen from the front c1909 showing the large duck pond.

Anyway there were an old man used to work with me when I first started work, we called him 'Cuckoo'. He could just talk like . . . just sing like a cuckoo. He used to make rhymes up and he made a rhyme up about Percy; he were a big feller were Percy, he said:

'Old Percy Wormald is very, very tall,
He drinks a lot of beer and it goes against the wall.
He'd drink a lot more if he wasn't so poor,
And now he hawks greens from door to door'.

There was a feller up at yon end pub; they called him Wilson Ward. He had a horse, and he used to cart coal, hawk coal. He had a bit of land and he used to grow a bit of clover for his horse, but when it was ready to lead he always had to get somebody to help him, he never could do it hisself, so this old man that I worked with made a rhyme up about him. There was another Ward what lived at this end of Back Lane, and if ever you were goin' by he always wanted to know where you were going. He always wanted to know folk's business and they called him 'W H W' – William Henry Ward. Well this old man made one up about him. He said:

'W H W (not Mr Lloyd), his manners are rude, his actions avoid,
He's like a boar pig, as fresh out of the sty,
And he's grunting at everyone instead of going by'.

'Five men in a boat'. Probably taken in the early 1900s, featuring Mr Maltby from Hull (Mrs Wormald's relation), at the tiller. Mr Richard Lambert and Mr Tom Booth (bridgemaster), oarsmen, with Herbert and Percy Wormald (brothers of Charles Wormald). Percy is the one wearing the bowler!

The old man what I worked for, first year I was with him, he got some bullocks. We used to take them onto the Common and one of 'em used to clear off to t'wood; jump out of the field and go into t'wood. Well we lost this bullock for ever so long, so old Gilbertson what I worked for, put an advert in the paper to say that he would give anybody a pound that could find him this bullock. Well, there was a little man in Back Lane called David Hall. He said somebody had told him it were a pheasant, so they were going to get it next morning. Well this old Cuckoo who made rhymes up went next morning in good time, took a horse and cart, and he got the bullock and got back before David had a chance to go. Well anyway, Cuckoo made a rhyme up about him, he said:

'David Hall is very small and I've oft heard people say,
He had a pound to catch a beast and lost it by delay'.

'Courting'
Aye, in them days when church and chapel used to be leaving together, you'd have thought it were a big picture-place leaving; you couldn't get down the

Horse-drawn wagon. One of the shooting parties regularly held at the farm in Bernard's time. Two of the Wormald family in the foreground obviously starting young!

street for folks. When we left church on a Sunday night we used to go down Ferry Lane over the bridge there, and you couldn't get down there for folks on a Sunday night – lads and lasses. That's where you used to start courting, down there meeting lasses and having some fun with 'em, I mean when we were young we had to go to church three times on a Sunday: Morning service, Sunday School and then again at night. In them days, t'Old Boys' School was the Sunday School, and I tell you, you couldn't get down the street for folks in them days.

Cawood railway station

That were a good little place, were t'station, there was some traffic there, they used to send some stuff out of there every night. There used to be a train on a morning, quarter to nine for passengers. On a Monday there were one at twelve o'clock, and another coming back at four o'clock, and then one at twenty to eight. Ordinary days there were only two for passengers, one at quarter to nine, another at twenty to eight at night and a goods train at three o'clock. Train used to take t'post, letters and that. A woman used to take 'em there in a bag and they used to put them on the train, and t'papers used to come back, an' all. Folks used to bring stuff from Kelfield and all them farms at Kelfield and Biggin, and there *did* used to be some stuff. There were two men on the station – porters. One was an oldish man who lived up at townend and the other was a good strong lad. They generally got them off the Wolds 'cos they were strong. And they *had* to be strong to lift sixteen and eighteen stones of barley and wheat offen t'wagon up onto t'dock, it used to take some lifting. Then they used to load on bales of straw and hay and they

Cawood Railway was opened in 1898 by the Lord Mayor of York. Passenger services ceased in 1929 except for excursions – Sunday school trips that continued until the mid '40s. Freight continued to be carried until the mid '50s. The station was one of Bernard's favourite places when young.

used to put a lot of wood on at the station, they used to fetch a lot of wood from Moreby, big trees. There used to be three wood-wagons, with three horses apiece in, and it were summat to see them horses workin'. They knew their job; they hardly had to be spoken to.

Flour mill on Thorpe Lane
There was the old mill down t'new road there, it were a flour mill and two brothers had it, Thomas and Matthew Smith. Matthew were Keith Taylor's grandad. They used to make flour there and when we were lads we used to go and ask 'em for a bit for frumenty. They used to give us a bag with this wheat in and we used to take it home and our mothers made it into what they called frumenty. We used to have milk on it and sugar, and have it for our supper, it were grand. Then they went bankrupt, in t'First War, and I remember I asked me mother what they meant by bankrupt, and she said: "Oh, they've lost a screw, a nut, and they can't get another, they have to get it from Germany". Well there were a war on you know, and you knew you couldn't get it from there and then they pulled all the machinery out.
But afore that, when they used to make flour, there used to be a Jew come from Leeds, and they'd have a week, day and night, making flour for the

View of Thorpe Lane showing the flourmill and, almost opposite, the Primitive Methodist Chapel, also known as the 'adult school' in Bernard's time. Both now demolished to make way for housing.

Jews. When they filled a bag, this old Jew used to put a ticket or some mark on it and then it was for unleavened bread like, for Passover bread as they called it. They used to put it on at the station and send it to Leeds and then when the Smiths went bankrupt they took all t'machinery out and had it for tillage for a bit. In t'First World War they had German prisoners in it and I should think they'd have about two hundred and they had to go out to farms. If any farmers wanted them, they had to send somebody to come for 'em, and take them away and then bring 'em back at night. They used to take them out on a Sunday for a walk, a drove of 'em, and they all had patches on their backs, on their legs and all over, to tell they were prisoners. They made a chocolate factory of the mill once. Well they made chocolates there, and by! we used to get some do's with the waste, you could buy it cheap. Then it went back again to t'tillage job and after that somebody else started to make it into a flour mill again but they never made much on it.

Gas in Cawood

And then there was the Gas House in Sherburn Street, t'old Gas House. An old man called William Shelton used to look after it and in the First World

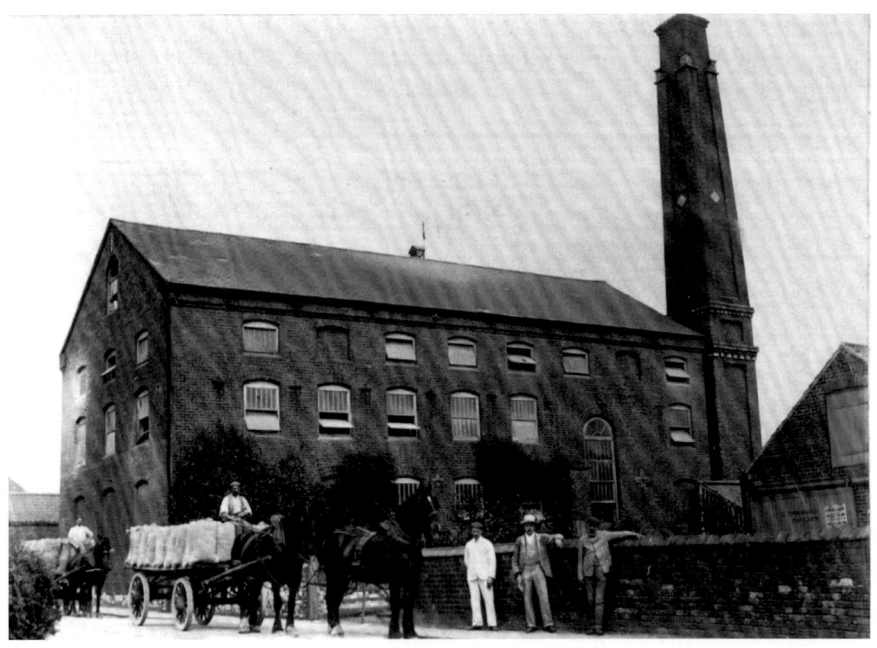

The flour mill on Thorpe Lane during its working life. Here it is seen in all its pristine glory. Later, in strong winds, it lost about two yards off the top of the chimney which ended up in Mr Burley's greenhouse next door. The mill had a varied life, being used at one time as a chocolate factory, after being a flourmill and later a cornmill grinding corn for Weetabix if rumours are correct. Then, according to Bernard, it was used as a billet for POWs in WWI. It also served the Army in WWII.

War when Zeppelins were coming bombing, they used to turn t'gas off, and we knew then that there were some Jerries in. If it were summer we used to get up and go into Back Lane and sit there and you could hear when they dropped bombs; you could hear t'old pheasants croaking out in t'woods and you could hear t'ducks up at the Castle ponds, they used to be croaking out. Joan Shelton's dad and her uncle Fred used to go round on a night with a long pole with a light in the end and they used to light all t'lamps, street lamps and then after so long it went bust and they'd to do away with it. Then folks got some lamps in t'shops and in church and chapel what went with petrol and you had to pump them up, and they had *them* for so long. When we were lads we used to go catching sparrows, 'riddling' as we called it. We used to turn 'em into t'shops, and first thing they used to do was to fly straight to the lamp, and away used to go t'bulb [mantle], and then they used to run [chase] us, and that's what we used to do, in them days.

Still more odd characters
Aye, there were some queer characters in Cawood. There were some queer 'uns in King Street. There used to be four or five houses where that feller's built that slipway. [Now gone since the flood wall was built.] Tom Warrington used to live in one of 'em, they called him Pom-pom, and Mrs Laycock used to live in another. Liz Brumitt, Norman Brumitt's mother used to live in one and an old woman called Mrs Taylor lived in another. We used to call her 'chinny' 'cos she had a queer chin, they said she'd had it burned when she were young. Then there were an old man called Nathan Tommery, he were blind. This 'Mrs Chinny' used to go stickin' [gathering sticks for her fire], and when farmers had their grass fields down by the riverside, they had to fence all up afore they turned stock in but as soon as she went, if she wanted some sticks, stile and all t'lot had to go! She allus had a saw with her and a bag and she used to saw down what she wanted, she didn't bother about it being fencing.

Then in Rythergate there were an old man called Tommy Wiseman, and he had a son called Arthur. This old Tommy Wiseman, he were once at Escrick woodyard; they used to go peeling trees, big oak trees to get bark off. I think they used to use it for tanning and that. One day old Lord Wenlock comes up to him and he says: "Where do you come from, my good man?" Tommy says: "Cawood, me Lord". He says: "Oh that awful place, Cawood". He says they used to nail him with his pheasants. You know there *were* some poachers in Cawood in them days!

Then when you go round there by Raymond's [Garbutt's], where Andy [Dalling] lived, there were an old man, they called him Josie Lewcock and they would listen to him on a night when he used to be fastening-up to go to bed because he used to be nailing his door up. Then he'd put table in front of it, and then he'd put chairs atop of that. Next door to him where Charlie Burley's wife lived, next to Stanley's, there used to be an old man called Turner, and we used to call him 'Wack-up', 'cos he used to go to t'old woman who lived in t'row, and he used to say: "Wack-up [wake up] Mary me lass, it's eight o'clock". So we allus called him 'wack-up' and they called him Jim Turner, and he had a little old man who lived with him called Taylor, and they used to call him, what were it now? Bantoft, Billy Bantoft Taylor, 'cos there were another Tommy Taylor lived up Sherburn Street. I forget what they used to call him.

Aye, and in Threadgold Lane there were some queer 'uns. There were an old woman, they called her Bessie Liddle. She once went into t'druggist – they

Cottages in King Street, Cawood. These ran from the end of the Ferry or Commercial as it was once called, along the riverside. Mrs Harriet Hunt (Addie) is seen as a young married woman, standing outside her front door. Her husband was a successful salmon fisher. Addie will be 100 years old next year (2006). Next door, nearest the camera, is the cottage where Tom Elcock (Pom-pom) lived. None of the cottages remain.

called it druggist then, chemist's shop, when some other women were in. I think it would be Doctor Lambert's uncle Hardy what had it then. This old woman she were very hard of hearing and she goes in and she says to him: "Oh, I want summat for our Bob, he's bunged-up". So when these women went out, old Hardy says to her: "You mustn't say that, you should say he's costive and bound". She says: "What! Cost a pound", she says. "If he never shits no more I won't pay that!" She had another son, and they called him Tommy . . . Billy, Tommy Billy, Tommy Billy that were it. He'd a hump on his back, and he were real hard of hearing.

Then next door there were a woman and a man used to live . . . Tom Fletcher, and then next door to them there were three men lived there; Bob Appleyard, Harry Appleyard and Bob Brown. Harry Appleyard would touch you to borrow a couple of bob now and again, and then he'd say: "When you owe anybody owt, you don't want to harass, because *they'll* be harassing plenty, so's it's no good *you* harassing".

Well anyway, one on 'em were taken bad and died and they took him to Selby, I think it were Bob, brother Bob Appleyard, and they're sat waiting. Somebody had gone to fetch him to bring him home in t'coffin, they allus brought them home night afore, carried 'em upstairs, and let them stop there while they buried 'em next day. And they're sat waiting, is Bob – Bob Brown and Harry Appleyard – and all of a sudden a picture dropped! Well, they always used to say if a picture drops it's a sign of a death to come. Well this picture drops and Harry Appleyard shoots out of t'house shouting "Which bugger's next?"

A village custom
When anybody died in t'village, the undertaker allus used to either go or send somebody to a man called Billy Lupton, who lived again t'church and they used to ask him to 'put the bell in'. He used to toll the bell for so long, maybe for ten minutes and then he would stop. He used to stop for a few minutes and we used to say: "Listen, see what it is, a man or a woman or a bairn". Then he'd start again, and he would give it so many bats; so many for a man, so many for a woman, and so many for a bairn and they allus used to say if a bairn died there'd allus soon be three other deaths, but I don't know whether there is. Anyway they gave over tolling the bell a few years back.

Medical care and transport
(Bernard starts a conversation with one of the children)
There would be two doctors in the village then. There was old Doctor

Cemetery Chapel. This was eventually demolished, the cost of repair putting it out of reach of the village. For many years it had only been used to store equipment, bier etc. The bell was rescued and preserved near the flats in Chestnut Road.

Walford, he were a big tall thin man and I never saw him ever have either a pony and trap or even a bike, he always used to walk, and he used to live in that house against the Anchor. Burleigh House is it?

Child: Yes that'll be it, yes.

Then there were another doctor called Doctor Ross, he lived down Church End where Danny Sykes lived, Ousebank House. He used to have two grand ponies and he had them a groom. If anybody came for t'doctor in the night or any time he'd to get up had t'groom, and he'd to get t'pony out and into the trap, and then he used to have to take him wherever he'd to go, and maybe he would have to wait long enough for him. They called him little Doctor Ross. And his wife died, I've heard 'em say she choked with a bone.

Child: A bone?

In her throat, aye, and then he married his . . . I don't know whether she were the housekeeper or t'maid. He died when he were only a young man, and they're buried at yon side of the cemetery there. He had a lass called Cissie, and a lad called Angus.

When Doctor Scarborough first came to Cawood, after t'First World War, he used to come on a bicycle and then he got a car, and it were like a . . . we used to call them 'biscuit tins'. They'd a motor bike engine fastened at the side and he used to put a handle in and when he used to turn it to start, he nearly used to lift it off its wheels. Then Mr Boyce, the school gaffer, he had one the same and they were just like a square box. They'd about a four and a half horse power engine fastened to the side with a belt or summat on it and they used to have to stick a handle in and start 'em up like that. They'd no cover on, no, nowt like that.

Child: Only two with cars in Cawood?

Oh aye and one was Doctor Scarborough's. There used to be one doctor lived at Burleigh House but I think it were before the First War and he used to get drunk, and he came to the house once, when your great-aunt Sally were born. They sent for him to come to Ryther you know, across there, and he must have tumbled in t'dyke as he was going, and when he got there and got up the stairs to your great grandma, he got sat on a chair at side of the bed, and he started taking his things off.

Mrs Kettlewood (Isy) speaks: And he was going to get into bed . . .

Aye, he were going to get into bed next to your great grandma and your great grandad used to say: "Our Sal were the cheapest bairn we ever had, we never got a bill for her!"

Then after the war, t'First World War, he came back and he lived at Burleigh House.

Corner End
You know when I first started working, all the men and young men used to make up to Corner End on a dinner-time and after tea on a night, and they all used to stand at Corner End. Us young 'uns used to sit on the saddler's shop window until they used to send us off or we'd stand there and talk and folks used to have to walk right round us. They used to grumble and then t'bobby would come and stand on the corner; he'd stand it so long and then he used to shift us on. Well, when he weren't there, some of us used to have a go at point duty, waving cars on and things like that. I know there was once

Corner End, Cawood. Here seen as Harris's. Bernard remembers Richardson's the saddler's shop being here. This is where the youngsters used to congregate, in the centre of the village.

a man called Jack Nicholson and he had a go. Well, he stopped cars coming by the Castle and then he stopped them coming by the bridge; he had them lined up, two or three here, two or three there and then he turns round and he walks away and sets off home, and he says: "Help yourselves".

But we often used to have a go at t'point duty job. I were once stood there and an old woman and a man comes in a car, and he pulls up at t'Corner there. She gets out and has a look and sees there's nowt coming and then she waves him on, and she gives us a good telling-off, but we did used to have some laughs there. Older men used to stand at t'bridge foot and they used to be watching for salmon going up when it were salmon time, 'cos they used to fish for salmon up in the marshes and they used to be watching for 'em jumping. When they were going up river, you could keep seeing 'em jump and some of them old men such as Georgie Rayner and Dan Denny and such as them, they could see 'em just with any bit of a ripple.

Sherburn Street as seen from Market Place. Bernard's family home can just be seen on the extreme right of the picture. They had a shop at the front and a bakery in the back. The 'Free School' as Bernard called it (now Bank House) can be seen on the left nearest the camera, then a butcher's and the Jolly Sailor. Mill House faces the camera.

Sherburn Street

I were born in Sherburn Street and I were brought up there. Folks allus used to say that Sherburn Street were a queer place, 'cos all t'women used to be out there callin' [talking/gossiping] on a morning by seven or eight o'clock, you know. The men used to go to work; some of them had to be at Olympia at six o'clock at morning and others would go for seven; they had to bike to Selby and be there for seven o'clock. Their wives used to be stuck outside callin', and they always used to say it were a place for callin' was Sherburn Street, but there were some good sorts in Sherburn Street, they would always help one another. I know one woman, her husband left her and she had three lads; he used to come home early on a morning and catch her in bed and he once gave her a good hidin'. Well, he allus rode a racing bike and when he were going away, the women out in t'street set about him and one of them shoved a brush shaft through his bike wheel, that tipped him up! They didn't half give him it! They wasn't bad sorts in there. A lot of them women used to go out to work you know. [Often work in the fields.]

Milk dealers

I can remember a time when I've fetched milk from five or six places in Sherburn Street where folks used to keep a cow. There was somebody where Pilmer's is, he once had some cows there and on the other side of the road, they kept cows there, too. There was an old woman where Mrs Hunt lived; she used to keep a cow and I can remember when I were only a little lad, going there for milk. Then there was an old man up where Jimmy Worrell lived, by the 'go-lane' [snicket to Back Lane] and he was a rum old stick. When they altered clocks first time it were for summertime, but he wouldn't change his milking time and we used to be going at nine o'clock at night in summer, fetching milk, 'cos he wouldn't start to milk until the old time, it didn't matter what they said. He used to have a little pony and trap and a real good dog and he used to tend his cows on t'roadside. He would set off there by the pub, t'Bay Horse, and he'd go right round by Long Lane and he never used to get out of the trap. If the cows went into a field or owt, that dog had 'em out in a minute. He used to go right round by Long Lane and he'd just to get back down Bell Lane and he'd be home for t'night. And by! He was a rum old feller.

Some lads used to have to go (and *I've* gone), right to what's the Experimental Farm now, fetching milk from there – Thompson's. And you could get it at the Grange, Mrs Nicholson *she* used to sell it; old Silver [Mr Silversides] he used to sell it; Mrs Hind used to sell it; Warringtons at Ferry House used to sell it; Hornshaws later on, they used to sell it; Harold Taylor, the barber, he used to sell it. Oh, there were somebody in every street used to sell milk in them days, they'd no restrictions nor nowt of that. Some on 'em were clean and some on 'em weren't. Old Bob Shaw wasn't over clean.

Fishing

You know two or three lots used to salmon fish, and they'd fish for some years and they wouldn't get hardly a salmon, and then a few years back they had a real good do, there were hundreds of salmon, I've seen 'em. I once saw eight in one net, just across the river, on t'other side of the bridge. They used to fish here along by t'boatyard, a bit further up there. For that there, they used to have a great big long net, oh about a hundred yards long and about eight or ten foot deep, I think. They used to have sinkers at bottom, and some corks at top, and they used to go so far up river, nearly to the bend at Wharfe mouth. Then one man used to row the boat out; he used to have the net on a board at the back of the boat. One of 'em would start and row across and the other would walk on the bank-side with a long rope to the net and he'd keep pulling it off. He'd go about three parts way across river with the

Mr Walter Elcock showing a fine catch of salmon. In 1929 a licence to fish for salmon cost five pounds one shilling (£5.05p), and the fisherman had to be named on the licence which was limited to two persons. If another name were added, there would be an additional charge.

Harriet Hunt (Addie) standing in her husband's fishing boat, with the net piled on the backboard.

boat and then when he got down to where Binks's field is [Northingales], he used to come in real sharp. They used to have all the side of the bank levelled off and the man in the boat used to jump out on to the side and then he'd start to pull t'net in. The other man what had hold of the back end with the rope used to let it come steady – allus were coming *with* the water, never against it. We used to sit and watch him and if there were any fish in, you could allus see when he were getting to the last part 'cos corks would dive underneath and then up again. They had like a little truncheon and they used to kill 'em with that, and they used to catch salmon of sixteen, eighteen, oh up to twenty pound. I've heard tell of them getting fifty pound. But I never liked 'em; I always liked it out of a tin best!

Return to Sherburn Street
If you'd have reckoned up all the families in Sherburn Street when I were a young 'un, I think there would be over two hundred in t'families. There were some real big families down there then, and you know all the stuff coming to the station from over the bridge and from the castle used to have to come down Sherburn Street. I've seen them leading cartloads of turnips day in and day out for bullocks at the castle. When it got to spring, they used to come and bring them down the street – bullocks, twenty of them, maybe twenty-four at a time, to load them on at the station; they used to put about ten or twelve in a wagon. Then they used to bring pigs and things like that. It were all horses and carts down Sherburn Street in them days. When you got into Back Lane there was old William Gilbertson and his sister Ellen at Chestnut Farm. You could go there and buy eggs, you could buy a stone of taties, and you could buy 'set' taties. They used to fetch straw from there for pigs and when folks had pigs they used to have all the muck to lead out and they used to skell [tip] it up in the street and then they used to shift it with a horse and cart. It all had to come down the passages; some hadn't a passage; with some of them it had to come through the house, all their coal and their ash pits, there were no water closets in them days. They all had ash pits, and they used to have to carry it out in bushels. I can remember when there was no scavenger here. Young Jacky Pilmer told me, when they first took the job on, they did it for eighty pound a year and then everybody had an ash pit, an earth toilet. There weren't above half a dozen water closets when I were young, and they used to have it to carry out in bushels. It were a thankless job.

When you were going down the Ramper, we used to call it Ramper down on Sherburn Road there, there used to be a footpath at the side of the dyke, with big stones in it, and they said it went right to Sherburn. Well, all on the

Scavenger cart. As Bernard says, "It were a thankless job".

other side where the council houses are, they used to put big middens there. Castle farm used to have great big middens along the side of the road there, and they used to be leading it there for days out of the fold. They used to leave it in the midden and then put it into tatie rows. They all used to put muck in the rows in them days and then women and old men used to shake it out, and then they used to plant their taties at top of it. They never have owt to do like that today; they never give it no muck. You couldn't get down t'Ramper there at the right side for middens, everybody had a little midden who had any land down there, and then they used to have it to lead up. It used to be a queer job if it were slippery for the horses coming up onto the road. I've seen 'em tumble many a time.

Bishopdyke

We used to go to Elcock's shop and buy a couple of hooks, fish hooks, and then we'd get a sinker or a lump of lead and about two or three yards of band, [string] and we'd go down the side of t'dyke and look for holes in t'side. Then we used to drop the old sinker just at the side of it, to let the worm and hook go just again it and we used to pull great big eels out, a couple of foot long. We used to spend all our summer nights playing there, and getting wet-shod. We used to jump the dyke when we were young 'uns, to see which could jump it best. There used to be two big posts there just again' them houses at yon end of Sherburn Street and we used to call them King and Queen and it was which could jump biggest. We've jumped in many a time. It were nowt to see a lad tumble into t'dyke and have to go home wet through, and they got a good hiding then; they aren't like they are now, petting 'em and going on. When they used to mow the weed in t'bottom of t'dyke, we used to put a piece of wood across or some stones again t'old pump, and get the weed to stop there and it used to come sailing down and packing up ever so tight, and then we used to walk across it. It used to hold the water up, and then the dyke men used to have to come and it would take 'em ever so long with a fork to get it out and then it all used to go into t'river and when we used to be fishin' at Race End [where Bishopdyke joins the river] with rods, it were allus in your line, raffling it up.

Jetty and work on the river

There used to be what we used to call the jetty there where Johnny Buckle had his antique shop [now gone], and there used to be a steam crane on lines, and in the spring of the year there used to be barges coming up loaded with muck for farmers. They used to have big pans with a bottom on hinges and then it had a catch on. It used to hold about a quarter of a ton of muck. Farmers used to have to come with their carts, and it were a rum job, having

Jetty. This is where a great deal of activity took place in Bernard's day. Tillage was stored in the warehouse near the jetty, which has now been converted into a private dwelling and is now 6 Old Road.

to stand on the cart and knock this bottom out and the horse maybe uneasy if it were a young 'un, it wouldn't stand. It were a dangerous job were that and a chap used to drive it called Tommy Warrington, he lived over the bridge there in t'first house. They used to bring fertiliser up, tillage, and store it in that big place of Johnny Buckle's what he had his furniture in, it used to be two storey high [now 6 Old Road]. Men used to tip these here big pans up, two of them, and they used to bring so many bags out with t'crane and run along metals up to t'footpath there, and then there used to be men there, and they used to carry it in. They used to have bags over their heads to keep it out of their neck-holes, like a hood and I've known a time when they were leading muck out of there they used to take it to the Anchor. There used to be a weighbridge there in Market Place [also one in the railway station yard, both long since gone], and they used to weigh it. Maybe one or two farmers, maybe three, wanted so much of it, so they used to have to weigh it. And I've seen the road down Old Road and up the new road [Thorpe Lane] and in Market Place, when it's been paved with muck from what they were leading. They used to say that the old muck-men at Hull used to put the hosepipe on it all weekend to make it heavier; it were nowt but sawdust and oranges and apples, there wasn't a lot of goodness in it.

A man called Jim Lund used to have a barge what used to bring a lot of muck up there. He lived where John Burley lived [15 Water Row] and he called this ship of his Wilhelmina; it were a grand barge, an iron 'un and he allus had it grand and clean and painted. He had a daughter called Wilhelmina. He only had that one daughter, I never remember his wife. She [Wilhelmina] married Keith Taylor's uncle George and they lived in London, and when Zeppelins used to come in the First World War I know they had a baby born, it was the only one they had. She were born deaf and dumb, she never could talk but she were a real grand lass and she used to go all over t'place. She travelled all over, and she never could talk.

This Jim Lund had a brother called Oliver who lived here near the vicarage. He had a threshing machine and the woman who used to run the Anchor was his sister, and when they used to be weighing-out there she used to come out to see, and she'd say: "You aren't right on the weighing". Maybe if the horse was awkward or if the cart had one wheel partly off the weighbridge she knew, she used to come outside with the book, and she knew whether it were weighing right or not.

Anyway, they did away with this jetty, and they used to bring stones. They used to dig two big holes and they had a gantry for the ship, and they used to wheel stone out. I've led it from there for roads. You used to have to back your cart into these holes, and then they'd a big gantry stood on a trestle. I used to have a good young feller wheeling out in a barrow with just one little wheel, and they used to wind it up did two men; they used to have a derrick onto the mast and two men would be at t'end winding it up. They had baskets, big baskets, and they used to have men in the hold, filling them. Then they used to wind 'em up and put it on this barrow, and you had to be a good hand to walk the plank. If you didn't get a proper step in, it used to come in and hit you on your feet and over you went, maybe into t'river. I've seen many a basket of stone go off the gantry because if it started going and he held tight to it he went an' all, so he used to let all the lot go, and barrow and basket of stone and the lot went. When the jetty was on the go they used to lead coal to the brickyard and to the gashouse.

Housing
There'd be just under a thousand, population. And there's been, I think, a hundred and sixty new houses built since t'war, and today, population's just about a thousand, it's never altered a lot in seventy years. But today you know there's only two or three in a family. When I were a lad there used to be oh, up to seven or eight in a family, plenty on 'em with twelve. There'd be fifty houses in Cawood what only had two bedrooms. How did they used to go on with all them lot? They had to fit 'em in somehow. But you know as soon as ever they got left school, they were off to a 'place'. Lads were hired onto farms and lasses went out to service at big houses, farmhouses, doctors and such as that, and that's all they *could* do. Today, there's some folks have a three-bedroomed house with two kids, a lass and a lad, and when t'lass gets to be seventeen she's wanting a place of her own. By gow! Them lasses in my day would have given owt if they could have *stopped* at home.

Farming
Just before the Second World War, there was as many as thirty farmers in Cawood, men who had maybe just a bit of land, maybe twenty acre and one horse. And they could make a living on it. Today they tell you you can't make a living if you've two hundred acres, but them men used to make a livin' in them days, and there was about thirty big and little farmers in Cawood. Today's there's six! [How many now, three?] And still there's all the land there, but you see the big men's got more. In them days there were more men worked on Castle farm than there does on all the lot today, a lot more. I mean today there's many a farm with four hundred acres and they only have two men, maybe their own two sons. They've been saying for years there wouldn't be any men to work farms. They don't *want* 'em today. I mean I talked to a farmer and he said one day last year they started at eleven o'clock and they did twenty five acre of barley, combined it, and got fifty ton of corn. It would have taken us five days to thresh that lot in our day! We should have had it all to thresh after we'd led it, cutten it, stooked it, and led it, and then it were all to thresh. We used to do maybe ten to twelve ton of corn a day. I mean they don't want folks on farms today. There isn't another industry what's done better with less folks.

The smells
You know before the Second War, you could set off again the station, near the Bay Horse, you could come down Sherburn Street, and you could smell the pigs and the horses, or summat in your nose all the way. You could go up to t'far end of Wistowgate and it was just the same. And going down Rythergate, you could allus have the smell of cattle or summat in your nose,

but today you can't have owt like that. I mean in Wistowgate there used to be I think seven farmers, little farmers. There isn't one today. No, you never see a bit of straw down there!

The river again
You know, there used to be a good bit of salmon fishing years gone by, and the old men when they'd had a good catch, they'd have plenty of money and they would go to the pub, and they'd give the old landlady a fiver, five pound, and they'd say: "Tell us when it's done", and they'd go on boozing, and then they'd say to landlady: "How are we going on then missus?" She'd say: "Oh! You're a pound into t'bad", and then for some old fellers, the landlady would have a slate, and she used to write down what all folks owed her. I've heard 'em tell of old men getting their handkerchief or a piece of cloth, and they'd say to one of the bairns there that they'd give 'em a penny to go and rub t'slate clean, and then t'landlady didn't know how much they were owing.

"It's nowt but catchment what's done it!"
Catchment's starting to build a flood bank here. Well, you know when we were lads we never had floods like there is today, it's nowt but catchment what's done it! I mean George Liddle . . . he lived yonder where Dick Liddle lives at Wormwood Hill, he lived there until he were about thirty two or three when he left, and he left about same time as t'catchment started round here. He went to Escrick, and he said he never remembered ever having water in t'house when he lived there. His brother took it, [the farm], the missus's dad took it and then Dick's had it, and they've had it [the river] in, I think, fourteen times since then. It's nobody but catchment what's caused t'bother. I mean there were houses that I knew yonder on t'landing what's been knocked down, there were five houses there. Well I never remember them ever having water in. It's catchment what's done it, they've cutten all t'trees down, they've letten water come faster. I mean when I were first married, if we'd had a lot of rain missus's dad would look at t'paper and if it said there was a lot of water coming over t'bridge at Otley he knew he had twenty four hours to get his beasts off the land he had at Wharfe Mouth, where the Wharfe goes into the Ouse. And then as catchment started, he used to say he could only give 'em *twelve* hours. Yet they will have it that it isn't them, catchment, that's done it, but we've had more flooding. Why, I never remember it in any houses when I were a lad, it's only been since they started messing about cutting all the bushes down at the side of the river and doing jobs, making t'banks higher. We never had a bank burst until about three years after they'd been at it. 1933 I think were the first time we had a bank

burst, and the banks weren't half as big then as they are today, and not half as strong. They'd never been touched; I never remember 'em being touched when I was a lad right up to 1929. Banks used to stand it then because we never got t'weight of water.

Bob Warrington who lives in the Croft in Fostergate, he said he was born at the Ferry pub in King Street and lived there, I think twenty seven years, and he said he never remembered water being in, and I know the first time it was in, Greens had the pub, Walt Green's mother. And Bob come to see it, and he said it were the first time he'd ever seen it in there.

Shopping
You know in them days you could get owt you wanted in Cawood. If you wanted a suit making you could go to the tailor where Pullein's shop is now. [Now closed] You could get a pair of boots made where Alwyn Lambert lives. His dad used to make some good boots, and he used to sell 'em an' all. There were shops for owt you wanted. But today there isn't trade for 'em, they can go away [to shop]. There used to be an old carrier and his wife who lived in Sherburn Street called Jackie Horner; they were a grand old couple, they'd bring you owt. I've seen folks go to them and give 'em a paper with some measurements on and say: "Will you bring us a suit for our so-and-so?" There used to be a feller called Corker who used to come into Selby market again the banks there, I've had suits from him, my mother used to take us there. Mr Horner would bring you owt you wanted. He used to go to Selby on a Monday and I don't know whether he went on a Wednesday or not. I don't know whether he didn't go to York on a Thursday and a Saturday.

I've gone with him to York many a time on a Saturday, I used to go and stop at me aunt's. You used to have to be ready for nine o'clock in t'morning, and off you used to go. When you got to Yeoman's farm, what's Stones's farm now, he would stop there and he would go up to the house would the old man, to see if they wanted owt fetching from York. They used to bring shares and things for ploughs, and owt they wanted. He would go to Bushells or Kay and Backhouse's and bring pieces of implements and that, and while he were up there, the old woman had a little bit of paper and she had a few crumbs in it, and there used to be a robin come and sit on the railings, and she used to feed him. Then when you got setting off, you were meeting roadsters [tramps] all the time, allus a lot of roadsters then, you never see any now. There'd be two of them, one walking at one side of the road and one at the other, and they'd be picking tab-ends up. Now when they used to see the old carrier man they would stop him and they'd ask him for a match and he'd say that they were 'abide with me'. He meant they were them safety matches what you could only strike on t'box, so they had to have a light and that were it, they didn't get two or three spare 'uns. I know we used to set off at nine o'clock on a morning and we used to get into the Lord Nelson in Walmgate about twelve, we used to put up there. If I was coming back with him I used to ask what time had I to be back there and he'd say three o'clock. If I weren't coming back while t'following week I'd ask him if that was all right and he'd say it was.

We used to set off back at three o'clock and he used to be calling at all the farms there were, all the way back bringing them stuff. He'd have a heck of a load of stuff for t'chemist at Cawood and when we got to Stillingfleet he wouldn't let t'horse pull it up the hill, so he used to have to stop again the church, and his missus used to look after the horse and he would go to George Redshaw's for help. Maybe George were doing summat else, maybe in the field and he would have to wait ever so long for him coming and we used to get to Cawood about nine o'clock at night. By gum, it was a slow job! It wasn't so bad in summer, but it were a rum 'un in winter. Two bits of old candle lamps at the side of t'old thing. Aye! and he wouldn't hurry t'horse wouldn't old Jackie Horner, no. And then he once got fined because horse'd turned a bit lame and somebody, a bobby, stopped him and he had to leave it! Aye, poor old feller he was in a bonny way because he wouldn't hurt a fly. Then he started a little shop there in Sherburn Street, and I know somebody had given him a coin with a hole in for a shillin', and he'd not seen it. So he screwed it down to the counter and he said: "I'll see nobody else is taken in with it".

Bricklayers, joiners and blacksmiths
Aye, there were a big family of Elcocks; they were all bricklayers and good bricklayers an' all. And then there were the Elcocks what had a joiner's shop and the Grand Hall. That were a rare place! It had the best dance room there was for miles round here, and two billiard tables, and a house to it, and a big dining place up at t'top. They used to have concerts there and they could have dinners and things. They said it were selled for five hundred and fifty, and t'house in, 'cos nobody wanted bothering with it, but by gow it were a grand dance room!

And I tell you there were two or three lots of joiners and there were two good blacksmiths – Marshall's they were blacksmiths, they came from Oakwood I think. Renee Marshall's dad were one on 'em and her uncle and I think it were her grandad, would come from Oakwood and I think he would be t'carrier for so long. When folks wanted to be in his caravan when they were going to Selby or anywhere, and they wanted to go with him, he used to say: "Clammer in" [Climb in] and when he wanted 'em out he used to say: "Clammer aart". [Climb out]. I know Albert Marshall were once umpiring a cricket match and somebody appealed for one of t'fellers, and he says: "Aart". (They used to say, "aart" for "out".) Feller looked at him, and he didn't know what to do, he didn't know what he were talking about. So Marshall says: "Aart", he says: "Come aart silly bugger, tha's yards aart", and so they allus used to call him 'Art' after that.

Pumps, plumbers and piped water coming to Cawood
There were allus two good plumbers in Cawood. Now you never hear tell of a plumber today. There were two good plumbers; I believe at times there were three plumbers. There was an Acomb, but he went to live at Appleton Hall, I think he got a job there. In them days you had to have plumbers because nearly everybody had a pump and when t'leather used to get worn on t'bucket, they used to have to have them redone. I've seen 'em off with things tied onto their crossbar, off out to farms. They had no water pipes nor nowt like that, it were all pump, and you'd see 'em going doing other jobs; they used to put glass in if a window got broken, a bit of painting and jobs like that, but most of their time they were mending pumps, 'til we got water.

I can remember water coming to Cawood, well, nearly everybody had a pump. And I mean when we were at Sherburn Street on a washing morning in summer, if water were getting a bit short, we used to have to go down to t'pump at town end yonder, and fetch two or three buckets o' water afore me mother could start to wash, or else we used to have go down Josh Middleton's yard where t'bobby's gone to live, and fetch it from there out of t'Bishopdyke. Oh aye, and lots of folks used a pump *after* water come in. I know Smiths in Sherburn Street used to have a tap at end of t'passage but they never had it in t'house, they had a pump and they wouldn't use owt else, and there were some bonny skirmishes when they said they had to have water in. A whole lot on them wouldn't have it. I know Isy's grandad kicked up a bonny row, he didn't want water, he wanted t'pump. Aye! It used to be a bonny goin' on and I know when anybody got it in, first set off, us kids used to go, and they would get a glass and they'd give us a drink and a lot on us, after we'd had it so long, we started breaking out with scabs round our mouths. Oh aye, it were a queer goin' on with it.

Horses, cows, milk and muck
You know every house what you would call a detached house in t'village had a stable, you see they'd a pony and trap and such as that. I know when we

Sherburn Street again, this time showing the village pump, or as Bernard says 't'pump at town end'.

lived in Sherburn Street, we'd a big place with a loose-box, then we had a stable and a pig sty right at t'end of t'garden, and everything had to come out into Sherburn Street. We used to get a wagon of coal at a time, and it were all to carry in bags, down into this place and we used to sell a bit when folks'd come. I know there were one feller who used to come from Biggin. He'd come for four stone of coal on a Saturday night, and he'd carry it on his back to Biggin when he went, and where t'old fish shop is, they would have a stable and Wetherell's had stables. Of course they had to have two horses for taking their stuff out. Oh, nearly every big house had a stable. A lot on 'em I think used to use 'em for hauling, for pulling ships up river, so they'd do that job. They'd have a little bit of land, maybe ten or twelve acre of land, and then they would do that job. A man would come and ask to be towed up to York or summat of that, and they used to have to go. I know Isy's dad used to tell us about when they used to haul, and maybe the man would have to walk right down Cawood Ings or so to fetch him, to pull 'em up to York. I've heard him say how they used to change horse across from one side of the river to t'other, and them horses got so as they could get in and out of t'boat sharper than the men could. But he said they once had a bad 'un; it used to jump when it got within a few yards of t'side. I think the boats had a bit of concrete in the bottom so's they could stand. And they used to be doing that at night, at any time, and that's what they had to do afore there were any tugs. I've just twice seen them hauling up the Wharfe. I once went with them to take a load of coal, a ship-load of coal to Appleton Hall, and then I once went with 'em to Button Hill with a load of muck for Warrington Brothers when they lived there.

Oh aye, and nearly every biggish house in Cawood used to keep cows. They used to keep one or two cows, and then you see you used to get your milk off 'em and then when the cow went dry you'd to go to somewhere else. There'd be seven or eight folks in t'village where you could go get your milk. You didn't stick to one. I know I used to go to one who used to take lodgers in and I'd go maybe half past eight in the morning afore I went to school and she'd set me on toasting for these lodgers. And she used to tell me not to touch it when it wanted turning. I don't know whether she thought me hands were mucky or what, and when I got back home I'd about five minutes to get across t'Cut to get to school. Oh, she were an 'eller for that.

I wonder what kids would say today, if they'd to go like Frankie Green and Ted Ward and such as them, and I've gone on a night too, right across to what's Experimental Farm now; it were John Henry Thompson's then. Mrs Bussey there in High Street, it was her mother. I've fetched it from there many a time. We used a lot of milk with baking and that, and I used to go for 'old' milk, they used to call it, for baking with. And Ted Ward and Frankie Green and them used to have to go right across t'fields. You used to go to yon end of the Ramper at that stone bridge, and then you used to take in across a field there, and then across two other of Thompson's fields, and that's what you had to do. They'd have a fit if you'd telled them to do that today would kids, by gow! She were a good old sort were old Mrs Thompson. When it were cold and you were off across, she always had you in and let you get to t'fire while she got you it [the milk], and then she'd give you a bit of biscuit or summat. I once remember she had some Jews used to go, and they used to take her some of this unleavened bread, Passover bread, and she would give us a bit. It were like, just like . . . what is it? Biscuits . . . like . . . these 'ere hard biscuits . . . they were like cream crackers, that's what they were like.

You'd think today there isn't fifty acre of grass round Cawood. Well, before t'Second War I sh'd think there were five hundred acre of grass round Cawood. You see folks had to have grass for their cows and things like that and their horses. I mean all t'little farmers had a horse, but they hadn't a grass field and they used to have to, what they used to call jist. [Joist] They used to jist here in Stanley's fields again t'cemetery, and in that where there's bungalows in Anson Grove. An old man called Blake, he had that, and there'd be four or five of 'em would put their horses in, and then maybe one or two would have a cow in. I can remember George Taylor's dad, Keith's grandad, he . . . I can once remember he used to keep a cow in that field there where Anson Grove's built, and then they used to milk it at t'side of t'road. There were some buildings where Gary Stead goes into his house there, and I've seen cows stood at t'end of them buildings on t'road and while they've been milking it, it's been eating out of a bushel. Aye, and it never used to bother. O'course, you maybe never had a motor car pass while they were doing that, it'd only be horse and cart, that's all it would be. I mean they'd to keep a lot of grass for their hay for their horses and such as that and they grew that much stuff for their stock, all kept bullocks. They thought you couldn't farm if you hadn't some muck, but today they can farm without muck, there's plenty of them farms that never have a fork-full of muck. I don't think these young 'uns would want any. They're not like George Liddle, he used to like to see 'em there, bullocks and that, but Tom and them and other lads, I bet they'd kick a bonny row up if they'd to 'fother' [to supply with fodder] on a Sunday like we had to.

I've seen Harry Frankish and them at t'Castle yonder, before they got an engine to chop turnips, they'd have hundred and fifty bushels of turnips to chop for beasts, slice 'em up, and it *were* a job 'til they got t'engine. I remember when they got t'engine, they had to chop on a Saturday, they hadn't to start engine up on a Sunday. Well, today they can't farm if they don't farm on a Sunday. But I mean you get such as George Liddle, his son, he's as good as any, he's as big as any in t'village, and he never turns out on a Sunday with owt and they still get it done same as t'others.

In t'old days you know, they wouldn't even take horses out on a Good Friday. *We* never used to, we used to work 'til dinnertime, but we never took 'em out. I've heard Isy tell a tale about when they were at Ryther. They used to sprout some taties in t'kitchen you know, and they'd a flat cart and a pony. Well, he wouldn't fetch pony out, so he sets t'flat cart up for t'lasses to carry these boxes out of t'kitchen and put 'em on t'cart. (They'd be getting over-sprouting and he'd want to take 'em where it were colder to slow 'em up a bit), and he jabs some wood under t'cart so's it couldn't skell [tip] up like – it were only a two wheeler – and they were packing them on and one must've gotten over far to t'back, and up she went! Spilt all t'taties. By gow, they didn't half cop it!

Working hours
I can remember before I started working you know, when they used to have to work all day on Saturdays, and I can remember going to old Gilbertson's one Saturday afternoon, and George Taylor's dad, Harry Taylor were haggling about having Saturday afternoon off. Anyway they got it till they finished at three o'clock and horse men when they were out in t'land ploughin' in winter, would take some hay with them, and they would take a bit of summat to eat for theirselves and they would stop at dinnertime and loose horses out and let 'em eat t'bit of hay, and they would just have it for about ten minutes, and then off they used to go again. They used to have to work till three o'clock, and that were t'first start when they got it to three o'clock and a year or two after, they got it to Saturday dinnertime. I think they would get it to one o'clock and then Saturday dinnertime. Then we got it to half past eleven, but now they don't go. If they go on Saturday mornin' it's overtime, so they've got it like that. By gow, t'old farmers used to fight when they wanted owt like that! And oh, there was a bonny row over Lloyd George, with t'stamps and things like that. Aye, they didn't like it! I've heard 'em talk about t'old man I worked for . . . no it weren't, it were t'old man at t'Hagg. They said when he used to be payin' 'em, when they first got pound notes, he says he was blowin' at 'em and goin' on. They said he was frightened to death he were goin' to give you two!

You know, they think they're badly done to, do some on 'em today; they're always wanting this and wanting t'other. When I first started, I used to have to go on a Sunday morning at eight o'clock and at four o'clock to fother-up. Saturday afternoons I used to have to go at four o'clock, and then again at eight o'clock. When I got a bit older I used to have to do t'eight o'clock. And right when we were married, we lived where Clarky [Charles Clark] lives, and I used to go to church and then I had to come up there and get me wellingtons on, and an old coat and go back to feed up at Sunday night. Then I used to come back and change into me other things and walk right by t'police station to me mother's. [Now 8 Broad Lane] Well, I mean, there's no fothering or owt like that to do today. We never got no extra for it most of t'time, you maybe got two bob, and you went every night at eight o'clock to fother-up and then again at Saturday afternoon and Saturday night, and Sunday morning and Sunday teatime and Sunday night and you got about two shilling for it. By, they don't know they're born today!

When old Charlie Wormald were at t'Castle, he used to go up to Leeds two or three times a week, and he used to come home on a Saturday night with t'twenty minutes to eight train. He'd come off that and he'd maybe be halfkalied [tipsy] and all t'men would be waiting there just in t'yard, for to get paid, and then Tommy Stronach would come out and say: "Boss isn't going to pay while [until] he gets his supper". Oh! you were out there stood waiting. I used to work there a bit when I were a lad, on Saturdays and such as that, and we used to have to go just same and walk up to t'house with our hair parted and ever so smart, and then he'd ask how many days had you been. I tell you, if he were a bit kettled he wouldn't pay while he'd had his supper.

I've seen Freddie Hunt's dad standing outside of Wetherell's shop waiting to put t'shutters up. Every Saturday night they used to put shutters across t'windows; they'd slide 'em in at t'front, and when he got 'em all putten in, there would be somebody in what had gotten their money about nine o'clock. He used to reckon to close at nine, and there they were, runnin' to t'shop to get their bit of groceries and pay their bill and such as that. I've seen Freddy's dad many a time stood waiting to put the board across t'doorway, and when he'd finished putting things in he'd put a bolt through and Dalling or Hamling, whichever it were, would put a pin in, then he'd have 'em to take out at Monday mornin'. Aye, they'd a bonny goin' on with it, about twenty-eight bob, or thirty bob a week it used to be.

More farms, farmers and work in the wood
The Castle used to be t'biggest farm in t'village, and then there were Warrington's and Gilbertson's and there were Lunds, they were farmers and Wards. There used to be three brothers of Wards. There were Ben who lived up at Model Farm where Irwin Savage lives; Harry, who lived in Back Lane and Joss in Wistowgate but I can remember Joss living where Geoff Hind lives. Whenever it were shooting time, they never went anywhere without they had a gun with 'em. I know when we used to go up onto t'Common, we'd get there maybe be half past eight on a morning and old Ben would be comin' back, he'd been all round folks's land, he were always looking for hares. And whenever he shot at one he allus had two barrels, we allus knew it were him 'bang, bang'. They tell me he used to be a queer 'un at allus wanting to have his dinner fair on twelve. His wife weren't over strong and one day there were a woman there helpin' her and she said she'd cap him. When she saw him coming in off t'road down to t'house this woman met him with it! And that capped him, he didn't know what to say to that. Harry Ward allus had t'gun on his bike and he used to go round t'Common twice a day, and if there were hare anywhere there he allus, allus knew where it were. And Joss, oh, he were for ever with t'gun, he'll have had hundreds and hundreds of hares and pheasants and that. I've heard 'em say when he were bad, he

Pause for a picture! Threshing day in Cawood Castle farm stackyard which overlooked the River Ouse, where Cardinal's Court now stands.

had pneumonia just before he died, and they said somebody went up to the house and told him there was a hare somewhere, and he were goin' to get out of bed. Whether it's a tale or not I don't know.

And then there were the Warringtons, they were biggish farmers and Teddy Warrington, when I first remember him, lived where Tom Liddle lives, he had that farm. And then he got a woman I think as housekeeper and married her and bought Compton Court and they used to call it Rythergate House then. Anyway, when I first remember that, Keith Taylor's grandad lived in half of it, and Wood what were t'veterinary, lived in t'other half. Well, Warringtons bought it, Teddy Warrington. I don't know whether it were his missus or what, but they called her Mrs Compton, and then she had it christened Compton House. And then I think it were Archer what christened it Compton Court, and he were a rum 'un were old Teddy, he used to make you laugh. They said when he went to buy t'ring to get married, jeweller asked him if he'd have some spoons (they always reckoned to give you half a dozen spoons when you bought your wedding ring). Anyway, he says: "Aye, give us a dozen", he says, "because we're going to have a large family", and I think both on 'em were over fifty then!

I used to work with an old man called Arthur Arden. He'd been in farming but he'd retired but he used to help George Savage a bit and he used to come there when I were there. By! he used to tell us some good tales about when he were young. When he were first hired out at t'Hagg, first year out, he used to go home and then come back at bedtime to go to bed. There were a foreman there for old Jackson called Smith who were Jack Smith's brother and of course they used to come to Cawood. He'd another old feller used to be hired with him and they called him Tom Fletcher who lived at Threadgold at t'finish and he said they once carried a six gallon barrel of beer to t'Hagg and had it across a manger in one of t'places and they used to go and sup it and they supped it in a few days. Old Arden says when he used to go to bed, he had to sleep with this Charles Smith, Charlie Smith, and he said when he used to come in on a night in winter and he'd gotten t'bed nice and warm, when Smith were ready to get in he used to say: "Get up there you young bugger, let *me* be there", and he said he used to have to get out of t'warm place and into t'cold. He says he can remember when they used to have to follow t'tip reaper. You know, afore they got binders they used to cut it with what they called a tip reaper, and so many on 'em would have a patch and they had it to get tied up before t'reaper come round again. He said they were working away and they just had a bit to finish and it come on to rain, so this Charles Smith what were t'foreman, he says: "I wish it had kept fine another hour," he says, "we could have finished it". And old Arden says under his breath, he says: "I'm pleased it's rained". Bobby Harland's grandad he worked with 'em an' all.

Aye, old Arthur Arden used to work in t'woods, his dad were t'foreman. There used to be five or six on 'em worked in t'old wood, before t'First War, before they cut it down. He said Mr Wormald at t'Castle used to have to see about paying 'em, givin' them their money and that, and if he had any haymaking or clover-making and he wanted to get on and get it up, he used to fetch these men from t'wood and they used to have to help him cock hay, cut clover, and such as that, you see. And then, oh, they'd maybe stop till seven or eight o'clock at night, and all they used to get were a drink of beer, and maybe a bit of cheese and bread.

But that reminds me of one old farmer. He allus used to say about Noah's Ark, that's when t'clouds are running towards t'Humber. One old feller had some hay to cock and he says: "Come on, we shall have to gather it up, Noah's Ark's up". So anyway, they had to stop till dark, cocking this clover or hay, whatever it were, and then next mornin' there were no rain, it were a grand mornin' and then towards night, one of t'old men says to him, he says: "Hey, no more Noah's Arks tonight, gaffer!".

This old Arden he used to work in t'wood and then when they cut it down, him and his brother bought a lot of top wood and they got somebody what had a steam engine and a saw bench to come and saw a lot up, and they used to sell t'logs. There were some real hard wood, I don't know what it had been. He used to tell us that men used to come to buy these trees. They'd buy 'em standing in summer and then they had 'em all to peel; they used to chop round 'em and chop t'bark off, then they had 'em to fell at winter and he said: "By, t'axe used to bounce off them trees", he said, "it *did* used to be hard!" Anyway they bought a lot of t'top wood and they sawed it up and he said t'parson Mr Brookes, he were parson here when I were young, come to see if he had any slabs of wood what he could make some stands with. He had some bees and he wanted to make some stands to stand t'hives on and he said he selled him some of these, and he says: "By, if he has never sworn afore, I bet he swore when he tried to get a nail into them", he says, "they were hard"!

Isy's Uncle George, and a man called Albert Jackson met t'other afternoon and they got on talkin' and old Jackson were saying about how they used to have to work when they were lads. Uncle George, he's eighty six, and Albert's eighty two I think, and he got on about how they had to work when they were lads. Uncle George was saying he must have been a good worker when he were a lad because at sixteen-year-old his dad tried to take a farm for him. He tried to take yon farm at Nattresses, Woodend Farm up Sherburn Road and he said him and his sister were going to go to it, but they didn't get it.

An old man called George Harper had left it and Fred Ward got it. He had a lot of lads and we used to go there on a Saturday and go into t'wood with an old carriage to get firewood and the mother were a good 'un, she always used to give us summat to eat. Them lads used to bike to Cawood, three on 'em on one bike, half-size bike it was. Fred were t'oldest in t'three, and he used to ride t'bike; Dick used to ride on a cushion on t'crossbar and Chips used to have two steps up on t'back wheel and he used to ride on that, and they used to have to come to Cawood School like that.

Mac Lambert used to go to 'em every weekend and holidays. They used to live next door to 'em before they went up onto t'Common. He said their dad, old Ward, sent 'em to Biggin to t'pub one harvest time with a great big stone jug, half stone jug, or summat like that, on t'bike to fetch some beer and he says they come back, and they put t'bike up again Biggin Bridge, leant it up, and t'front wheel swung round and t'bottle flew off and into t'dyke and broke. By gow, that lad did cop it for that! When they left that farm they went to live at Melbourne and Mac said they set off at Saturday morning, soon on, to walk t'beasts, and they walked some beasts right to Melbourne. He says it were tea time when they got there. Aye, he said he were tired out when he got there.

Well, these old Harpers what lived there afore Wards, he were a little old lame man, and his wife, she . . . we had some Belgian refugees in t'First War who lived up at yon end o' Sherburn Street and folks used to give tuppence or threepence a week to help to keep 'em while they got goin'. This old Mrs Harper used to come and collect it on a Saturday night. I remember she had some false teeth, and they allus used to be rattling and clattering, by she did used to make a row!

Aye, you know that farm there at Wood End where old Harper was, it were swarmed with rabbits and I think t'man what used to take shooting at t'wood would be a colliery owner. Well, old Harper wrote to him and asked him if he would get rid of some of these rabbits like, because they were eating all t'stuff he had on t'farm. Anyway t'man wrote back and told him that when t'rabbits were on his land they were his and it was up to him to kill 'em but old Harper said he were killing as many as he could and he couldn't do no more.

Hiring
All them farms up there had a hired lad or two. Old Bussey, Pickard Bussey at Gale [Gale Farm] used to have a hired lad. Tindalls had when they were there; Busseys used to get three or four hired lads and they'd have a hired lad at Springwood and this here other place, Oakwood. I've known thirteen different folks be on that farm in my time. I know once there were some folks there called Skelchers and they had a young boy, he were a bit more than a baby, he were killed with t'lightning, and they always said it had gone in under t'door. I can just remember that little lad being killed with lightnin'.

Talking about lads having to get hired, well when I were a lad, plenty of houses in Cawood only had two bedrooms, and they'd five or six kids, you know. As soon as some on 'em were old enough they had to get 'em out because there was nowhere for 'em to sleep. It used to be a bonny going-on finding 'em somewhere to sleep, so they had to get hired and t'daughters used to have to go to a 'place'. They'd maybe go to farms, maybe to doctors or they'd maybe go to big houses. It gets o'er me today, how them lot would have liked to have stopped at home. Today, you get a family with about a lass and a lad and they've three or four bedrooms, a real grand house, and by t'time they get to be seventeen year old, t'lass is wanting a house, a place of her own, she's wanting a flat and such as that. I wonder how they would have gone on if they'd had to sleep four in a bedroom, or five on 'em, like they used to have to do, when I were a lad. I mean they don't know they're born today.

Lads used to have to get hired. They used to go to Selby on a Martelmas [Martinmas] Monday, and a farmer'd ask them if they wanted a job and if they agreed money, how much to go for, for t'year, he used to give 'em five shillings and they used to call that 'fastening penny'. Then maybe when t'lad talked to somebody else and telled 'em where he was going, they would warn him if they knew it wasn't a good place, so he would go and take t'farmer his five bob back. But some on 'em used to be good places and they used to go and they didn't reckon to draw their money while Martelmas, 23rd of November [Martinmas 11th], leaving date. Some on 'em used to try and leave all their money on and some on 'em used to have to have a 'sub', as they called it, to carry 'em through. As soon as they come home they used to have to hand their money over to their dad and mother, and then they used to have maybe a week or ten days at home and then they would either go back to t'same place or else they'd get hired again. And that's how they used to go on. By gow! They had a rough time on it had some on 'em.

They used to have to go miles walkin', they hadn't no bikes hadn't a lot on 'em. They used to set off in a gang and walk, maybe set off from here and one would drop off at Kelfield, another would drop off between Riccall and Kelfield and then right on till they got to Duffield, South Duffield and North Duffield and such as that, where they were hired. They'd no bikes nor nowt when I can first remember.

No, in them days when lads were all hired at farms, there'd be maybe one at a farm, and half a mile or a mile off there'd be another two, and they used to go and meet at one another's farms on a winter night. They used to sit in t'stable and clean their horses and plait their tails and such things as that, they never used to come away. They only got away on a Saturday night, and if they didn't get back in by ten o'clock at night, t'door were locked and they used to have to sleep in t'stable or in t'barn or somewhere like hay chamber or somewhere like that. I can remember once, one farmer across at Kelfield, he said men had to be in at nine o'clock. So it comes to harvest time and this lad were going up Kelfield Road there for another load of corn out of t'field, and he hears t'church clock strike nine at Cawood church, and he sets off back with t'rulley down t'road and he runs up to t'back door with it, and he jumps off rulley and into t'house he went. Farmer wanted to know what was the matter but t'lad told him. He says: "You said we had to be in here by nine o'clock and I'm going to be in". And he didn't know what to say, didn't farmer.

'Kids today'
They make me sick today to hear 'em say, t'kids, these young 'uns has nowt to do that's why they're doing all this vandalism. They say they've nowt to do. What about us when we were lads? We used to have to walk t'streets and such as that. We've walked to Ryther, we've walked to Wistow many a Sunday night after we've been to church. Now that's what, we didn't used to be breaking things up. If we'd have brokken things up we'd have gotten 'brokken up' at home, when we went in. Our mothers and dads didn't have money to throw about to pay for things being mended, or for owt you'd done wrong. If t'bobby catched you he'd flatten you with his cape, he'd hit you across your head with his cape and knock you down, but nobody dare say nowt. It's same with t'school boss. Aye! our old school boss would have straightened 'em up today, or else he'd have known what, and I mean he were at Cawood o'er forty years. He teached men what were old men when I used to work with 'em, and one said he'd teached him when he first came to Cawood.

Shops
I can remember two dozen shops. There used to be a little old man in Sherburn Street, he used to sell a few knives and forks, saws and spades, and things like that, called John Lund. And then me dad had his shop there again' t'chapel. We used to sell bread and stuff like that, pastry, and all sorts of things you wanted, pegs, pans, blacking brushes, all sorts, any sorts of things. Then there were t'fish shop, t'other side of t'chapel, fish and chips. Other side of t'road there were Bob Proctor who used to sell boots, and he used to mend boots. You'd get any pair of boots you wanted there, he used to have a shop full of stuff and then there were John Smith's, he used to sell underclothes and things like that, all women's stuff, and vests and shirts and that for men. And then at Christmas he used to set all up with Christmas toys. Further on there were Wetherell's, that were a big shop. He used to sell groceries, all feeding stuffs, bran, sharps, and cake for cows and all that. They used to have two men with wagons taking t'stuff out, or a man and a lad. The front of their shop used to be hung with rolls of bacon and hams and things like that, and when it were hot weather you could see all t'grease runnin' out of 'em. If anybody wanted any bacon, they used to just cut it. I

Shops. Wetherell's in Market Place showing rolls of bacon and ham illuminated by the sun shining between the Jolly Sailor and Mill House. The Anchor sign can be seen on the left.

can remember a time when they just used to cut it with an ordinary knife, and t'lads what used to work in that shop, they used to have to do all t'weighin' up, there wasn't things weighed up like there is today. That's why they cost so much today, 'cos there's so much to do with packing them and presenting 'em. Them lads used to have to weigh flour, currants, sugar, everything had to be weighed up and they had to get all the orders ready to go out into t'country. They used to send orders to Riccall, Kelfield, Ryther and Biggin and then men used to have to go to Selby twice a week to fetch stuff, wi' t'wagon and horse.

When you got to Corner End what's a butcher's shop now, Turner's [2 Market Place], that were a saddler. They called him George Richardson and he were a good saddler, he could make some good harness. Round t'corner were t'chemist. David Lambert's dad had it so long, but I can remember it when David's dad's uncle, Mr Hardy had it, and he were t'chemist. You could get your prescriptions, you could get owt you wanted there. David's dad were a proper chemist, and then when you went up Rythergate, that little house again t'Anchor doors an old woman called Bella Cleveland lived there. She used to sell goodies and make bread and stuff like that, and she made that bread what they used to have to take to church for old folks. There used to be so much money left every year for to find bread for old pensioners, old

46

Cawood Post Office and General Stores in the centre of the village.

folks in them days, and they used to go on a Sunday morning and collect it. Further up there were a chap called Copley, he were a tailor; he didn't used to do much but he could make a suit. Across t'road where t'doctor's surgery is now, there used to be two old women lived there, they were milliners, they called 'em Miss Firth and then further on there were a Miss Taylor, she used to have a goodie shop, and further on still there used to be her brother what's other doctor's surgery. It used to be a barber's shop, and they used to mend bikes and things like that.

When you went down High Street, there were a little woman there where Alf Abbott used to live, she used to sell goodies and make a bit of cake and things. She used to make pop and sell it, and you could go and get a glass for a penny. I used to go wi' Billy Wormald, the son from t'Castle what got killed on his motor bike. And then up on t'other side there used to be Bartle's grocer's shop, what's Turner's now, and then coming back there used to be Hind's, they had a bicycle shop, they used to sell bikes and tyres and things like that, and I think they used to sell petrol an' all, you could get it in a tin. Next door it were Alwyn Lambert's dad's shop. He were a boot cobbler and he used to sell boots and things. And then where Mrs Bussey lives, that used to be a little butcher's called Tommy Parker. Next door where Ella Neville lived, that used to be another butcher called Tommy Grundill. He were a real fat butcher were that, and then at Corner End it were Elcock's

Miss Taylor's goodie shop. Miss Taylor must have got married and become Mrs Clarkson by the time of this picture. Notice the school bell on the Old Boys' School that disappeared during alterations to the school some time ago.

Bartle's grocery shop in High Street near the bridge foot. Futher on can be seen Hind's cycle shop and Lambert's shoe shop.

shop. Mrs Elcock, Mrs Pollard's mother, kept it. They used to sell papers and pans and baskets and nails or owt you wanted there; biscuits and goodies, all sorts of stuff.

When you went up t'new road there were a little shop there where Wilf Storr's house is, that were Miss Carnell's and she had t'Post Office, and by she were a queer, fiery old lass! She used to sell goodies and biscuits, flannel and wool for knitting socks and things like that and if you went in and she were in a bad humour, by! she'd snap your head off! But it's all them what's had t'Post Office, they're all t'same. I mean when Mrs Pollard had it, she got while it were topside on her, she was as mean as owt when you used to go in. And then t'other feller what got it after them, he were t'same, Whalley. When Davis got it, well he's t'same, it nearly got him. He used to be as mean as muck when you went in. I sh'd think old Tommy Dixon will get t'same when he's been there long enough.

'Nowt to do'

You know, they make me sick when I hear 'em talk about there being nowt for young 'uns to do. When we were young there were a billiard room in

Sherburn Street with two billiard tables, well, when you were young they wouldn't let you go in, but as you got older they used to let you go, and you could have a game of billiards for tuppence, for twenty minutes. Well, if there were any big 'uns in, they wouldn't let you get on, and you'd sit in there on a night round t'fire in a place that they used to call 't'monkey cage'. They used to have it all fastened up with wire and that, and t'old man called Mr Elcock used to look after it. Then there was the Adult School where old Hartley had his furniture job. Well, all t'big men used to go there, shop keepers and school gaffer and such as that. We could never go in, they would never have us in there. They had a billiard table and a bagatelle. We had to make our own pleasure in them days; we used to go doing tricks in t'street, maybe tying somebody's door or summat like that.

Sport?
They allus had two football teams, but half of t'first team used to come fro' Selby and that's how a lot of these lads got into Cawood, they married Cawood lasses. Davis, Oliver and Sullivan all married Cawood lasses. They used to have two good football teams, and when you went there you could hardly get on t'far side line to get near-hand to have a look. If Jimmy Lawn and Billy Marshall and them were there and you went and stood agin them, they did more footballin' on the touchline then they did on t'field. They were kicking and punching you if you got agin 'em. Old Jimmy used to look

Football. A gathering of locals to admire and celebrate winning the Barkston Ash cup in 1913.

Cawood's cricket team c1920. Caught on film whilst gazing right, towards the official photographer. Back row from left: umpire, George Oliver, Frank Lister, Charles Hall, Tommy Cartwright, Herbert Hall, George Hall and umpire. Front row seated from left: Richard Morton, William Hall, Charles Jackson, Frank Thompson, Joss Ward, Harold Baxter.

at you and he'd give you a great big kick and then ask you what *you* were doing. And there were Billy Marshall, he were as bad. There used to be some good teams though, and there were allus plenty watching 'em.

When they'd a cricket team, they used to play cricket in t'Park, well it were only a little pitch and I can remember a time when old Joss Ward used to play. When they had to go to Micklefield and places like that, he used to take 'em in t'trap and t'others had to bike. I've biked with 'em to Micklefield. They had no fancy whites to play in; they were lucky if they had a pair of old grey flannels and they used to have one pad on, no gloves nor nowt like that. They used to have a right good team, generally finished up fighting at some of t'places. There were allus summat of that went on.

Winter
We never seem to have winters like we used to. I can remember when we'd always two or three days or a week or two skatin'. You could go down Ferry Lane, there on t'right-hand side all them fields used to be flooded, and you

could skate on all of 'em. You could go down the Marsh, past the church towards Wistow, and all t'left hand side there right up to Wistow Clew [Clough] would be all flooded. There were some good skating on there and there used to be some good skaters in Cawood then. T'old school gaffer, old Boyce, *he* were, and Frankie Ward who lived in Back Lane were a good skater and Hemingbrough from Wistow. There were a lot of good skaters in Cawood, but they never get chance to skate now. I've walked across t'river when it's been flooded, when it's been frozen over, but we never get any winter now, for to do owt of that.

Pig killing

As far back as I can remember, and that's back to 1910, they said all t'folks in Cawood used to keep a bacon pig, that's a pig to kill for themselves – a pig weighing owt from just under thirty to just over forty stone and some farmers would have them bigger, and them two little butchers what lived in High Street – Tommy Grundill and Tommy Parker – they used to walk miles killin' pigs for folks. They used to start in November and they'd be killing till March. Some farmers would kill seven or eight, but cottagers just used to have one. It were a day were pig killin' day! They used to have to have a copper boiling ready for t'butcher coming, and he used to come and get t'pig out and he used to knock it down with an axe; he had an axe with a thing on t'end and a chopper on one side and he used to knock it down, and then he'd cut its throat. Well old Tommy Grundill, he got where he were getting old and he sometimes used to have two or three shots at it, to knock it down. Well, when lads used to come home fro' school they used to go and look, and if he were there they used to tease him about having to have so many shots.

But anyway, when he got it knocked down, it were all to scald and to scrape all t'hairs off. Then they used to hang it up, take all its innards out and wash it all down. Then next day they'd come and cut it up. Well they used to cut it up like two hams and two big sides and t'head off. You used to have a rare do then. You had to start and take 'fries' out as we used to call 'em. You'd to get a dinner plate and you would take any of your friends and neighbours a plateful. You would take 'em a bit of liver, a bit of sparerib, a bit of chine and summat like that. When you used to take 'em it, they never had to wash t'plate. If they washed blood offen t'plate afore they gi' you it back, pig wouldn't keep, it wouldn't salt right.

Well, when you were going to salt it, you'd get a big block of salt, about eight inches square and about two foot long, and you'd this salt to cut up ever so fine into a bowl, and then you'd have to have about half a pound or a pound, of saltpetre. You'd lay t'pig down maybe on t'dairy floor or somewhere like that, flat, and you used to salt it, cover it all with salt, but you used to shove some of this saltpetre into all t'joints, all t'knuckle joints, because that's where they used to go bad if they didn't take salt right. And then you used to put t'hams on. Well, t'hams were always more particular, because they'd more bone in 'em and then you were watching to see whether it kept or not.

You used to leave it in salt, covered thick with salt, for about three weeks or a month, and then you had to take it out and wash it all, and put bands on it and hang it up. You could go in many a cottage and there'd be a couple of good hams weighing owt up to twenty or thirty pound, and these great big sides of bacon and what we used to call t'chap, that's t'bottom jaw, they used to salt that an' all.

That reminds me of a tale of an old farmer at Ryther. He'd made more space by hanging chaps up in his attic, and there was this little Tommy Lund, he were working for Charlie Elcock, bricklayer, and they were pointing up in t'attic. Old Johnny Gilbertson comes and he asks Tommy if he likes pig chap. Tommy says: "I do". Then Johnny says: "Aye, *I* do". Tommy thought he were going to give him one, but there were no such luck!

Healthy eating or 'It's riding about in cars what kills folk'
What I say is, today folks is always grumbling about cruelty with keeping pigs and hens and things like that. Well, it's only folks what's wanting it *lean* what's cruel, because they won't eat no fat, they want lean. Well when you want lean you have to half-hunger 'em to death, and that's where all trouble starts. They start fighting, picking, biting, all sorts. I say it's folks what wants stuff lean what causes bother with such as that, and I think this . . . it's a lot easier to feed pigs and give 'em summat to eat and make 'em go lie down and get fat, than it is to feed lean, and that's where all t'fault is today. They say that you don't want to eat fat, and you don't want to eat this and that, well you can go into cemetery and there's folks there eighty and ninety that's lived off fat bacon and taties – them Gilbertsons, Stockdales and all them. They'll have eaten more fat bacon than anybody.

No, when you had a pig of your own to kill you'd allus summat in t'house, as they used to say. I know we allus had one, and you could go and have a good slice of ham, and such as that, at Sunday for your tea. This rubbish you get now it isn't worth eating. I mean, you don't get as much grease as'll fry an egg today. Before, it were running down your chops like I don't know what. I mean today, well, if you don't mind [take care] how you cook it, there's nowt left in t'pan. You'd good pork pies as well when you killed your own pig, and they *were* pork pies, they weren't half bread.

You see, what cottagers used to do, they used to kill their pig, and then maybe at Martelmas [Martinmas] when t'lads come home, they would maybe buy 'em two more young 'uns, to start off again. They used to start with two, and keep 'em till t'middle of summer, and then maybe they'd sell t'gilt. They always used to like the hog to kill, because if it were a gilt you had to be careful and not kill it when it were in season, or else it wouldn't keep. That were a job, trying to get your pig salted right, so's it would keep. I've seen one keep two or three year, and bacon as good as ever. I've seen when they've been cooked, when I were with old Gilbertson, they used to cook half side, half o' two, and there wasn't a streak of lean in it. It were just like pink, that's all it were. And old Miss Gilbertson, boss's sister, she never touched owt unless she licked her fingers, she were frightened to death she were going to loss a bit of fat, and she lived to be eighty some. There's plenty o' folks in Cawood, poor folks in bad times when it would have been a poor job if they hadn't been able to go and buy a basinful of dripping, as they used to call it. Some of them kids were brought up on dripping and bread. They'd get a good basin of dripping for fourpence.

You know nowadays they tell you you don't want to eat fat, you don't want to eat taties and such as that. Well, you can go and look in t'cemetery and see these old folks, and old farmers and that, how old they lived to be. Well they would eat plenty of taties, plenty of fat bacon and that. I think it is that folks don't get about plenty, they sit in cars o'er much today, that's what's matter with 'em; old folks used to walk miles and miles. There's some Stockdales yonder in the cemetery, there's four of 'em on a stone, and they're getting on to well over three hundred and fifty year put together. And I'll bet they ate plenty of bacon and plenty of taties and such as that. I think it's all bunkum. It's riding about in cars what kills folks today. I think most folks would have lived as long in t'olden days, it's only them what died of consumption and such as that. I mean there's a gravestone where there's three lasses died. Well, I think they all died wi' consumption when they were only about in their twenties, but there's plenty of folks round 'em lived to be ninety and such as that. I think it's all wrong this here about not eating fat and taties. Look at Irishmen, they used to live on 'em, and who were any stronger? Who did any more work? I mean they used to live on 'em when they used to come across to help with harvest and hay time and picking taties and that. They used to put a pan or a bucket of taties on to boil wi' jackets on, and all they got were that and some bacon.

Apprentices
You know in t'olden days Cawood lads used to have to go for 'prentices, say joiner, blacksmith, builder, and they used to have to go for seven year, and they got nowt, they just lived-in, they got their keep. I've heard Mr Garbutt, Raymond's dad, say he were hired at Stillingfleet. He was apprenticed at Stillingfleet first, and he didn't like it and he came here to where they live now. Wilf Storr's dad had it, and he come to be apprenticed with him. They'd to do it for seven year, and they never got any pay, and they'd all sorts of jobs, and he said at weekend when he wanted to go home he had to walk to Aberford. He said he used to go across t'fields. And I've heard old Arden say first year he were hired out, he were at t'Hagg, that's just agin home, and t'next year he were agin Hazlewood Castle. And he says his dad used to set off and meet him on a Sunday morning, walking, right through t'wood and across by Biggin, and Fenton and to Barkston, through there, to bring him his washing.

And after, when they went to be 'prentices, they could be what they called 'bound'. They used to get two or three pound then, and they got two or three pound when they finished, about a fiver altogether. I think, it were some charity what left it for 'em. You know there were a lot of charities in Cawood; there's some for bread, there's some for coal, where they can give folks a bag of coal at Christmas, old widows and such as that. There used to be one . . . yon house at Corner End [Bank House] opposite t'Post Office, that used to be called t'Free School. Well, that were for anybody who'd lost his wife and had some lasses, they could go there. There were an old woman there called Miss Sidwell she used to teach 'em, they never went to school, all they did they went to church on a Sunday morning. They used to wear blue straw hats and blue capes. I can remember about four or five on 'em there. There'd be this old woman, she used to teach them and look after them, and then there were another old woman used to cook. It were for kids in Cawood and Barwick-in-Elmet. Well, as soon as it came as nobody wanted it, they sold it. Rent from that farm just by Biggin Bridge used to help to keep it going, but I think now they give it away as a scholarship. If anybody passes this scholarship they get so much money.

School
You know in them days kids used to come in [to school] from t'country all the way from the Hagg and brickyard houses, right from Woodend Farm there. Oh, and from Ryther, Jaspers, Springwood, Oakwood, and Stockbridge, all them places there would be kids and they all used to have to walk while they got big enough to get a bike. There were no dinners at

John James Allison. Bernard's favourite milkman and much loved villager, seen here on his tri-cycle in Thorpe Lane giving a lift to Auntie Marian.

school for 'em, they'd to bring their dinners, and they got a drink of water if they wanted a drink at dinnertime. They'd school to sweep up if so be they'd made any crumbs, else they'd get into bother about it, and they never used to leave while four o'clock at night unless it were middle of winter and then he used to let 'em go at ten to four. And then they'd to walk. They don't know they're born today, they do nowt but get carried about. I mean finding them dinners [at school] and such as that! When we used to go in [at home] there were five of us went in for a dinner, and we allus had a good dinner. I don't wonder it costs all this money now.

Milk delivery – John James Allison
You know, I've talked about where you could buy milk in Cawood when I were a lad. Today there's none of that, it's all putten on t'step for you and t'milkman we have now, I think he's turning a bit idle. He brings you a couple of pints on a Saturday morning and it has to last you while Monday morning. He's a bit different to his father-in-law, what started t'business. I can remember poor John Allison, he'd be dishing it out of t'can when we were coming from church at twenty to eight on a Sunday night. There he were, there were no bottles in them days: he used to have an oval can with pint and half-pint measures hung in it, and then he used to dip in and give you what you wanted and then a little drop to spare. I can remember one night we were coming from church and it were snowing like mad, and he's telling a woman what he's dishing it out to, that t'next job he got he was going to get one where he could keep his hands in his pockets. He were a rum old stick were old John. He used to tell a tale about his lad wanting a dog, a pup that somebody had for sale. So he said the lad had better get it, but he only had five shillings and the dog would cost ten. So John said they would have it between them and he gave the lad five shillings. And he said one night t'dog were misbehaving so he got a stick and gave his half a good hiding. Then he said somebody opened t'door, and it shot out and took his lad's half out with it, and he said it were long enough afore they saw it again! He always had some queer cracks. He come up to me mother's one day, it were t'day afore Christmas I think it were, and he's talking to Matt, t'brother in law, and he said they were havin' a couple of ducks for Christmas. He'd dressed them the day before and took 'em into t'house and telled his missus to put 'em out of sight or anybody would think they were havin' a couple of watterhens!

Local preaching
You know, in our day, a lot of t'farmers were local preachers. My pal used to tell me about his dad when he were hired out at a farm at Ryther and he said

that his boss used to go out preaching wi' t'pony and trap. He'd maybe go to Sherburn, Milford, or he'd maybe go to South or North Duffield. He said he used to have to wait for him comin' home on a Sunday night, 'cos he had to put pony and trap away and he said he'd be sat waiting for him with t'stable lamp ready when it were wintertime. When he heared him come he used to go out, and he'd to loose pony out of t'trap and take it into t'stable and take its harness off, maybe give it a drink of aired water if it were sweating. And then he would have to push pony and trap into t'gig house, before he could go to bed.

There were one old farmer, I think he'd come from somewhere by Fenton, or Little Fenton and he were a bit of a tatie dealer an' all. He used to get into t'pulpit and give 'em a right good do there for about three quarters of an hour, and then he used to say that if anybody had any taties or peas to sell, he'd see 'em in the vestry after t'service.

Fair and feast
You know, in Cawood, they used have a fair and a feast, and t'fair used to be on twelfth of May, and t'feast I think it were either second or third week in August. There used to be roundabouts, coconuts, swingboats and all things like that. They used to have it in a field behind t'Bay Horse pub and when they gave up having it there, they used to have it on Gill Green. I've known 'em have swingboats and things like that in t'Market Place. They used to have swingboats up again that house what they call Mill House there. All villages used to have a feast, but Cawood had a fair and a feast, and I've heard 'em say when it used to be t'fair, they used to have cattle right down Rythergate. That place up again t'boatyard they always called that the Bull House and they say they used to put bulls in there. A lot of villages used to have what they called a feast round about and they used to have races, bike races, and things like that.

Music
You know in t'village they had two or three men and women who taught piano. There used to be a lot of kids who learned to play, and one woman, Mrs Baxter, she had a lad who were a good piano player and he used to play at dances and there'd only be maybe him and a man with a violin in t'Grand Hall there, playing. Then there were another man called Herbert Smith, he used to play. Well, he used to get half drunk when he went to dances, and all t'time he were playing, he used to play a bit and then he used to stop and he used to say he wanted more light on t'piano. And so they christened him 'Morelight'.

Herbert 'Morelight' Smith and bridgemaster Sid Booth near the cabin on the bridge. Bernard talks of Herbert playing for dances in the Grand Hall but never having enough light after having had a few drinks.

Fields

You know some fields in Cawood, oh, they had some real grand names. You never hear anybody mention field names now; we always used to talk about Castle Garth. We used to play in t'Castle Garth a lot when we were kids. When you went down the Ings, past the church, you just got by Goole Bank, and there were two fields there where they used to play football in one on t'left hand side, behind t'bank, and they called it Fletcherses. I don't know where that name came from: there were first Fletcherses and second Fletcherses. They used to be grass fields and I can remember going to see when they were ploughing-out and draining 'em. Then when you get further on, there's what they called the Hauling Road, and then there used to be one called Jackie West, and Jackie Farrar. When you get further on, and begin to leave t'road and go up t'bankside, they used to call that Fareswell, and they reckoned it were an old name that when Vikings came up, they parted there and some went back, and they called it Fareswell. Further on there's Wheel Hall, we always call it Wheel Hall but I think it's marked Well Hall. I wonder if it were Wheel Hall, because there's a big ness there, a big bend. Then there's Clew [Clough] and Ingwell; that were a little lane that went off Ings Lane, and it's called Ingwell, and there were some fields down there, they used to call them Ingwell. And then comin' back, there's one they called Captain Turner, it belonged somebody what used to have a ship, and it's called Captain Turner. Then there's Grass Crofts, and Dunsills down t'Marsh and Beevers and there's a field called Mill Hill – well that's highest part in Cawood, is Mill Hill.

Then there's Gravel Sheds, that were a big piece of land between Marsh Lane and Wistow Road, and Cow Pastures, that's down Oxfield Lane. Then when you come our way, where our bungalow's built, they called that Carnaby Close. Where Anson Grove's built, that was Stony Garth and then just further on up Ryther Road there's what we used to call Northingales. Well, some used to call it Nightingales, but I think the proper name's Northingales, because it's up north of Cawood, and I think its proper name were Northing Dales. When you go down Boggart Lane there were a lot of fields in there, but they've made 'em all into one now. Where those caravans were, that was Frank Stronach and then the next one were t'Brickyard, then t'Long Nathan, Silverhorns and Calf Garth. Then when you went into Fostergate, you come across Fewler Field. Well, I don't know where they got that name from and Rabbit Warren and Mountain Field, and then you've Barn Field, Fostergate Field, John Hall, Far Fostergate, and Long Field, and all them are made into one.

I don't know how they'll do with t'Ordnance maps when, if ever, they come to find fields, because there's about seven of one lot in there, there's seven all made into one, and there's five further on in Fostergate, that's made. There's Green Dykes that's down a lane off Fostergate, there's Moxon, Shoulder of Mutton and then there's Croft in Fostergate. There's where Jimmy Firn lives, and they called that Betty Wilson. They call where Peter Sykes lives, the Old Pottery; aye that's the Old Pottery there.

Where these bungalows are, where Mrs Curtis lives [Fostergate] there behind George Taylor's farm, that used to be called Treelands, there used to be an orchard in there, and that's where we used to go for apples when we were kids. There used to be a lot of orchards in Cawood; there was one again Goole Bank; we used to call that Berryguard, and it had a load of berry trees. Then there was a big one down Oxfield, there were one there, it would be two or three acres. Behind Sam Sykes', there's a little field in there what they called Tithe Barn, and if you look behind Miss Medd's house, there's some old buildings there [now gone] built in stone and they used to think they'd been a tithe barn where t'parson used to store his corn what he got from t'farmers in olden days.

Up Sherburn Road there's a field there at this side of Hooton's they call that Nanny Golden. I don't know where they get a name like that from and then further up, where young Green's bungalow is, that used to be . . . now then . . . Sand Wharf. There was a big pond there and they used to call it Sand Wharf. Further on there was a field where I used to work and it were called Farmer Moor.

Now when you come back by Irwin Savage's [Broad Lane] there's Hodgson Forest. And down Burley's Lane in Wistowgate, that used to be Nickey-Nackey and then in Nickey-Nackey there were so many fields and they called them Big Mois Acre: Big Mois Acre and Little Mois Acre. All them fields in olden days used to have names.

Rythergate farm
In Rythergate, where Ray Goodrick lives [now 4 Rythergate] that used to be a farm, when I were a lad, that were a farmstead there. There used to be two big doors and then a swinging door at t'top so that when they took a load of straw in, it used to push under it and a man used to keep two horses there. There were a little place at t'side where a saddler used to stuff his horse collars; he used to keep his straw in there, and he used to stuff saddles for horses, cart saddles and collars and that. Mr Louis Hornshaw, he would what

they call 'draw' some straw. He used to get bags of straw and draw 'em to take all the bent straw out and just keep the straight, and then he would tie it up and take it to t'saddler Mr George Richardson. He used to mend canvases, them were things for binders, what used to take t'corn up into t'knotter, into t'tie-er or binder and he used to mend them when they got torn and laths smashed. They used to put new laths on and mend 'em there.

When Ray Goodrick's dad [father-in-law] used to live there, he were a comic. He used to take milk out you know, and he once went to a woman one mornin' and he tells her he's had a bit of bad luck. He tells her he had some ducks in a place next to t'pig and one of his ducks had gotten underneath pig and t'pig had killed and etten [eaten] it. But then he says, it would have been worse if t'pig had gotten through to t'duck and t'duck had etten t'pig! And when anybody used to say to him about being a long while coming, he'd tell 'em he was summat else besides a milkman. He'd say he were t'brushhead puller-on, rug shakker and coal-bucket filler, as well!

Paddling in the Bishopdyke
When we were lads we always used to go wading in t'Bishopdyke in summer, and before they filled it in at this end, we used to call that the Race End, because it had been for a mill race we think, in olden days. There used to be a mill there again Mill House, again t'Jolly Sailor and it allus used to run fairly fast down there, but when we used to go wading we always had to put boots on when we got behind houses there, because there was allus a lot of glass and stuff. We used to lift stones up to try and get eels, there used to be a lot of eels, but when we used to get to t'new road, going under New Road, we used to allus have to start and get a move on, because I think there were some of the first water toilets in Cawood there. If you went to the toilet in some of them houses there, when you'd done, if you looked round you'd mebbe see ducks or a swan swimmin' by, you never had to bother to pull t'chain!

Days of old
Things has altered in Cawood this last few years. You see t'jetty's gone, basket maker's gone, mill's gone, station's gone, Castle farm best in t'village, has gone. And banks has gone, we haven't a bank now. We used to have two banks; we used to have two fish and chip shops, them have all gone. We can't get a chip shop now. We used to have a clock mender, we used to have a dentist who'd come once a week. We used to have a man come round who'd measure you for a suit and bring you it a week or a fortnight after, and a chap used to come round mending clocks. They used to come round

sharpening your scissors and your knives, and such as that. A man would have a funny sort of a thing with a wheel on, and he used to wheel it from village to village, and then when you wanted owt sharpening he just used to stand it down, put a belt on the wheel what he used to wheel it on, and pedal it with his foot.

Years ago, they used to have a gala at York. I think they used to have it about three days sometime about June or July. They used to have a balloon there, and they used to give folks rides up in this balloon and I think they had a traction engine or summat like that to pull it down with. They used to let it go up so high and then at night after tea they used to let this balloon go. We'd watch which way the wind were blowing and we used to say to me dad: "Shall we see t'balloon tonight?" And he used to look at a chimney to see which way t'wind were blowing, and then he would say: "Oh, I don't think it'll come this way tonight, not where the wind is".

Well, it used to come about ten miles out o' York, and then it used to drop. First one there used to get ten shillings, so there were an old woman one day, they called her Bella Binns, she would be Johnny Buckle's grandmother and she rushed up, and said: "Bella Binns, first man up". So she would get ten shilling I should think. I can remember when she died, Mr Buckle in Back Lane, old John Agar, it were his mother, and I was watching him making the coffin for her. We used to go to Kelfield on a Saturday and an old woman there kept a goodie shop and we used to have a penny to spend so we used to go to her. She were a grand old woman, I think they called her Mrs Archer, and I remember telling her that I'd seen Mr John Agar Buckle making a coffin for his mother, and she said: "Aye, I should think he shed many a tear over it".

Bus services
Me and Isy were watching Prince Charles's engagement on television the other day and I says to her: "Well, they wouldn't have had to do what we had to do when we got engaged". I can remember it, it's fifty four years since. We went to York on a Saturday; a feller had just started a bus service. He'd gotten an old wagon, and he'd built the sides up and putten a sheet over t'top and he'd a couple of seats down t'side, forms like, and then a little 'un across t'end. When we had to get in, he had a stepladder, about six steps and he used to throw it in t'bottom of t'wagon. When you wanted to be out, he used to let end go down and he'd hook t'ladder there and you got in and out like that.

Well, we got to York all right and we got the ring bought, and when we come home at night we come by Escrick. I couldn't reckon him up, coming by Escrick. Anyway we gets to Patterson Hill, that's that hill between Escrick station and Stillingfleet, and t'old thing wouldn't pull, engine were goin' and we weren't shifting. So he stops and he comes to t'back, and he says: "Will you get out, and give us a push?", he says, "Me clutch is slipping". So we had to get out. There were only me and Isy and about three or four women in and one of 'em were an old woman from Stillingfleet. Anyway he told her she'd better stop in.

So we started, and he starts her up, and we pushed and we pushed and I know by the time we got to the top of that hill I could hardly bend my arm when I wanted to get into t'bus again. And that were one of t'first bus services what started from Selby to York. I think they called him Brear, that man.

I can remember Stan Moore starting his, he started with an old Florrie Ford, and by gow, what a going-on we used to have in there on a night coming from Selby and going to Selby, when so many on us got in, and some lasses! It were one of them with wooden wheels, and a hood what used to let down. Then he got a little platform wagon, about a tonner it were, and he put a top on and a sheet over, and that's how the first bus services started from Cawood to Selby and York.

Those were the days!

I often wonder how they would go on now fetching beasts up, milk cows up, from t'Park to bring 'em home to milk like we used to have to do. I allus remember what a job it used to be, coming over Corner End. I can remember one of the lasses were fetching 'em up one day, and we'd gotten a new bobby; and there's cows coming round t'new road and there's a car coming over t'bridge, (I don't know whether it were o'er bridge or whether it were down Sherburn Street), and this young bobby . . . they used to stand at Corner End a lot, and they'd do a bit of point duty when they were there. Well, there's cows coming one way and a car coming from t'other and there's this young bobby. Anyway he put his arm up to stop t'cows, but t'old cow didn't bother, she kept on walking. I don't know how he'd go on now when there's traffic lights, it would be a queer job bringing 'em up.

There were another old woman that lived in t'village when I were a lad, they called her Mary Milner. She would have been what they call a midwife today, but I don't think she'd ever had an hour's training all the time she'd been at it. I think what she picked up she picked up with working with doctors at

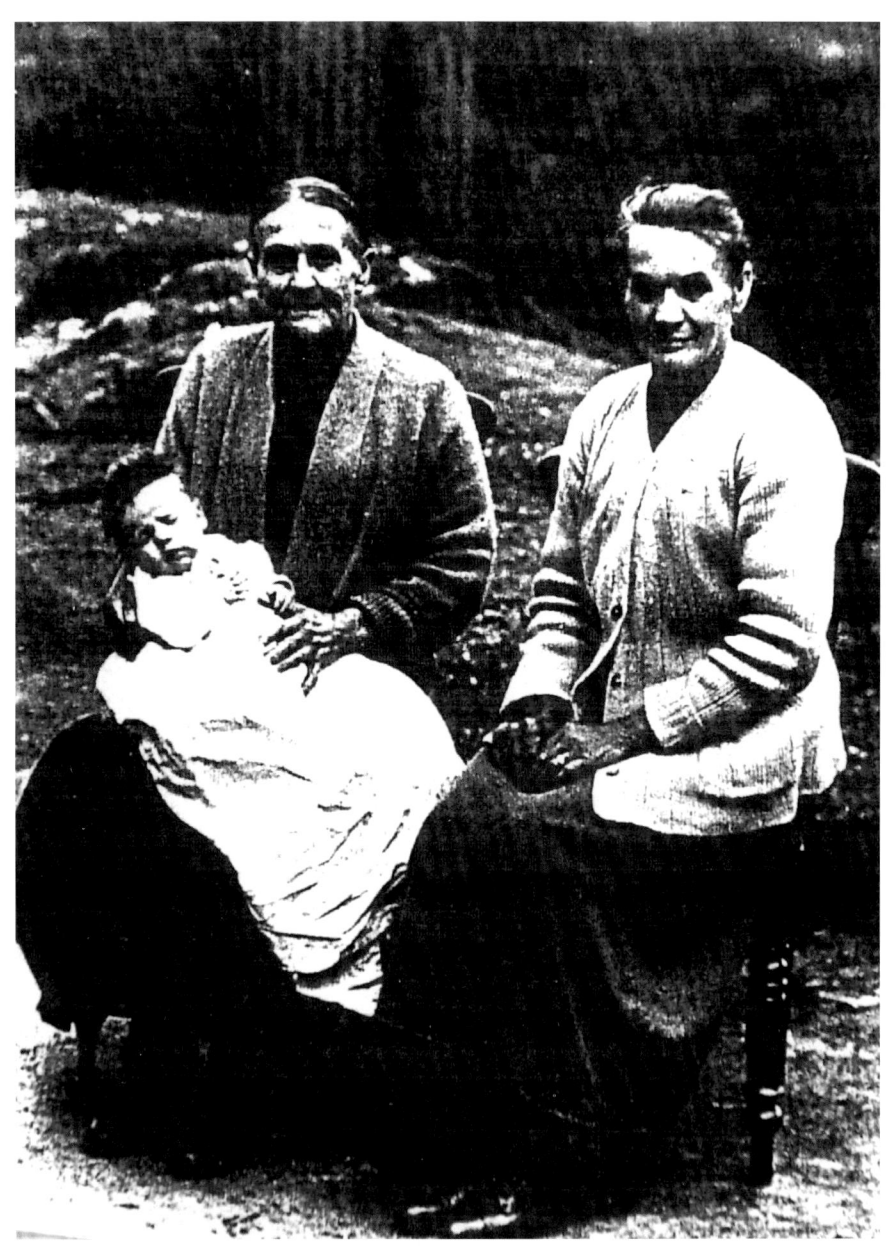

Mary Milner (née Lupton) born in 1852, midwife and village handywoman, much admired by Bernard, pictured here on the left sitting holding her grandchild with her daughter Ellen Lund. She was the person called upon at times of birth or death in the village.

confinements and that. And I know when they . . . [became pregnant] there were none of this going-on like there is today, running with their water to t'doctor to get their fortune telled! In them days, when they gotten their leg over they just used to go to old Mary and say: "I shall want you in so long". And she'd say: "All right Joy, I'll come". Then [when the baby started to arrive], she'd go. Instead of running to clinics and such as that, a lot on 'em were down at tatie pie, sorting taties out or down in t'tatie rows scrattin' taties. There were none of them goings-on in our day. And then again, if anybody were badly [ill], she were there, and when anybody died, she were there to lay 'em out.

On the day of the funeral she would be there. They used to fetch coffins to the cemetery on a bit of a thing called a bier, there were no hearses in them days, they couldn't afford 'em. They used to have this bier, and the man that lived at Cemetery Lodge used to come with it. It had no turntable on it nor nowt of that, you had to hook it round t'corners when you wanted to turn a corner. Feller at front used to have to lift and feller at back used to lift t'other way and they'd to go maybe right down to t'far end of Sherburn Street or right down far end of Wistowgate. You'd see them go into the house and then the undertakers would put t'coffin on, and old Mary would be there, bringing wreaths out and putting 'em on top and she'd have a snow white apron on. You didn't need one of them old English sheepdogs like them T.V. adverts to see whether it were white or not. They didn't have spin driers and things they have today; it used to be elbow grease and some soap, and then a rubbing board and a peggy tub and then into t'copper to boil. Oh, t'biggest job on a washing day were getting t'copper going. If t'wind were wrong way, they couldn't get it to go. That's how they had to warm their water in them days, they'd no immersion heaters and electric coppers; they'd to warm it with t'old copper and get some wood underneath to get her going if she didn't go o'er well.

Aye, in them days when there were a funeral, if it were anybody at yon end of Wistowgate and they were chapellers, they used to bring them to chapel; if they were churchers, they used to take them right down to church and then come back here to the cemetery. Years ago when t'little chapel were there in t'cemetery, what they've just knocked down, when it were on the go, churchers used to go into this side on it, it were in two parts, and Wesleyans used to go into yon side. When there were a funeral, old Billy Lupton what used to be sexton like, well he wasn't sexton, he were verger, he used to watch for the funeral coming up t'flagstones there at Water Row, down by Old Road and he would start to ring t'bell, toll t'bell, and he used to toll it while they

All Saints Church, Cawood, which played a large part in Bernard's life. How well he remembers all the various clergy who officiated there.

got to church and then he used to stop. When the service were over in church he used to start again when the coffin went out and he would toll it while he thought they were to t'cemetery. He'd do all that, and then when anybody died he used to have to toll it then. Undertaker used to go or send a lad, and I think he used to get a shilling for it, that's all he used to get. And the bier what they used to take coffins on is under a hedge here at t'back of Cemetery Lodge, I don't know what they'll do with it. [It was sold a long time ago.] Today they can afford a hearse so they don't use it.

When there used to be a funeral in Cawood, if anybody was passing with a horse and cart, he used to stop and go to t'horse's head and he'd take his cap off. If anybody went by on a bike, he took his cap off. If they were threshing either at Castle farm or Charlie Warrington's there again Pulleins, they would stop the machine while it got by. They were allus like that, they wouldn't do owt queer and they allus showed a bit of respect. And you could hear that old bier coming miles . . . well not miles away, but a long way off.

You could hear her rattling in t'hubs. It had wooden wheels with rubber tyres on.

Wistowgate
Wistowgate . . . I thought what a difference there is down there! There isn't a house down there but what's been renovated. By gow! it's a different look to what it used to be. There used to be . . . going down there, there used to be the Piperer, the old pond there outside Dr Dawson's [Ash Grange, 1 Broad Lane] what folks used to take their horses through to wash their feet when they'd been ploughing and were all mucked up. Farmers used to take their hard rollers in there when t'hoops were coming off in summer, to tighten them up and leave 'em stood in t'pond. And there were old Mrs Nicholson at t'Grange; well, she allus had these shutters across windows in this first room, and we used to say it were haunted. Poor old woman, she were about eighty year old, but I used to fetch milk from there, she kept a cow or two. Kitchen used to be as bare as owt, just an old mat down here and there, an old pricked rug, in front of the fireside, and there used to be Harold Hudson running about with a bushel of turnips and a bit of straw and that for t'cow.

Then there were Teddy Stockdale next door, where Blundells live. They had a horse and cart, and t'old man used to be walking about in his yard with a hard hat on and a walking stick and bent double, he used to be lame. They said he got lamed at t'jetty, at riverside there, and there'd be Ernest coming out with t'horse and cart, and his sister Alice holding t'gate open and shutting it after him. Old Ellen Firn lived across the road, Tom Turner [Sayner?] 's wife's grandad and grandmother who used to be doubled-up with working on the land. She must have worked until she were seventy or more, and they said she could pick taties, scrat taties all day just bent down and she were doubled up.

Then there were old Silver [Mr Silversides] at t'pub. Aye! a rum old bloke were old Silver. He used to keep a cow or two and sell milk, and he'd a horse and a bit o' land. Aye, I've heard them say he could spit across three or four fellers' knees and hit the fire to t'inch. He used to kill pigs; he used to do all sorts did old Silver. And then next door to what was his buildings, that were a house and George Hall lived there, Charlie and Bill Hall's dad. We used to go and play with them there, and they'd an old pram and I used to go with Billy [Wormald?], and they used to ride us up and down t'road in this old pram, and then across t'road next door to them, were the old Taskers, two brothers. They used to call 'em Sankey and Moody, they were both

Wistowgate. One of the very few photographs showing the actual maypole towards the right of the picture.

bachelors, and they used to do all their own work, all their own cleaning-up and that. I used to have to go and take them their bread on a Saturday about three o'clock, and they'd gotten all cleaned up and that floor . . . you could have eaten your meals off it! And their table and kitchen chairs were scrubbed white and the fireside black-leaded. They just used to have a pricked rug agin t'fireside and maybe a bag at the back door. Nobody helped them, they always did their own work. When I used to go, maybe when they'd nearly gotten finished, one of 'em would be sat in a chair and he'd have a cat on his knee. They always had two or three tortoiseshell cats.

And nobody lived in that house where Moores have altered it. They used to keep their apples and sprout taties and such as that in there, and then across t'road there were a woman lived there, they called her Mrs Harold Warrington. She were a widow. Herbert Wormald married her when I was a lad. Then Renders lived next door, old Bill Render, by he were a comic! It were as good as a pantomime seeing him get on his bike to go to work with his missus helping him to get on. She used to bring a chair out and he used to stand on it and she used to hold t'bike and then give him a push off, when he used to be going into t'dykes [to work in the dykes]. I think next door to them were, I don't know, I think they called t'old man Pocklington [Poppleton?], what used to live there. Then there were t'Maypole, where Stockdales lived. By gow, they've altered that! I went by the other night when it were all litten up, well it isn't same place. You couldn't get into t'yard for all the hens and turkeys and ducks when Stockdales used to live there. They used to have a great big midden against t'far back door. By gow, there's a bit of a difference now. There isn't a handful of straw in all Wistowgate!

Then there were Joss Ward, he had next place, he used to have a fold full of beasts in there, next door. They used to skell turnips up on t'roadside there, onto t'flags, and fork 'em through a little door-hole into t'turnip hole. On the other side of t'road there were George Lund's dad and mother, they used to live there, and they used to go down into Oxfield Lane that way. Old George Firn used to allus go that way into Oxfield Lane and across to Goole Bank. And then there was Arthur Lund's, they used to live where that over-fancy house is that's been all done up. They all had pigeon cotes; they used to have hundreds of pigeons there. They had a big pigeon cote had Stockdales and at Arthur Lund's, Goole Bank, Herbert Lund at station, all them. There used to be hundreds of pigeons around there.

Then there were a row of cottages . . . well, every one of them has been altered now. I think when they were selled all t'four would only make about two hundred pound, and they were asking five thousand for one with just one bedroom, a month or two back. Then there were some old folks who lived where Jim, what-is-it lives, what do you call him? [Wilkinson?] Old Neville used to live there, with his mother, and I've heard Isy say they used to take their chickens to market, I think they used to be carriers a bit. Stockdales used to do that an' all. They'd take your eggs and your chickens and things to Selby, and sell them for you. But this old Neville, he lived there, you'd see him when you went down Wistowgate, allus lookin' over t'gate, seeing what were going by. And then there were Prestons, they lived where Dennis Burley lives, he were a painter were old Preston. At t'other side old Sammy Bishop used to live down there, a little frail old man he were, allus lame. And then Bussey lived there, school boss, one of t'school teachers, but he died when he were a young feller. In 1916, last time I remember going to him, I went with me war certificates. When they used to sell war savings, he used to run it and I had to take it down there to him. I never saw him any more after that.

And then there were some folks lived where Gilbertsons live, I believe it were Ernest Button. He had a brother further on, further down Wistowgate called Johnny, and they were two brothers but they couldn't work together. They lambed together, but when they went leading hay or clover or owt, they used to take a ladder with 'em and fork up onto t'load while they could and then

The Maypole Inn in Wistowgate, this time without the maypole.

they used to carry it up. They wouldn't one fork and t'other loaden, like that, they couldn't agree. Old Baker lived next to where Dennis lives, where Edie lives [35 Wistowgate]. He used to take stuff to York, apples and taties and celery and all stuff like that. There used to be four or five on 'em out of Cawood. They used to set off at three o'clock on a morning when new taties were ready, and you'd hear them going over Cawood bridge, and they'd be coming back about three o'clock on a Saturday afternoon. Well, they used to go Thursdays as well. Old Jackie Pilmer used to go for years.

And across from where Edie lives [35 Wistowgate], them two big houses where Eileen lives, [Victoria Villas], Woods used to live there, and he were t'veterinary, were old Wood. And then Boyce the school boss, he lived in the other one where t'other lad of Burley's lives, who has t'garage [now replaced by houses]. By gow, he were a rum 'un, he would have straightened 'em up today! I never saw anybody what could beat him at school, he could put you in your place! And then where them bungalows are, Buttons had their stack yard. I've seen 'em threshing there many a time.

Horses having a drink and washing their feet after work at the Piperer, a pond at the junction of Wistowgate and Broad Lane. The Grange can be seen towards the back of the picture. Notice the little bridge on the left where the water used to run under the road. The pond has been filled in for many years. Some of us still miss it.

Then by Edie's there used to be four little cottages. And then t'next one, an old Mrs Moore used to live there and Busseys. I think maybe Edgar would be born there . . . well no, he maybe wasn't born there, but he lived there so long. Then there were four cottages. There used to be an old man called Hoss Lightfoot lived in t'first one. He once told me he carried corn for thirty days, and he could carry corn could old Hoss. In t'First War he said he carried it for thirty days and they would be carrying sixteen and eighteen stones in them days, and then there were a Jackson lived there, and by! he allus had some good singing birds. He once had a thrush; it's the only time I've known anybody what could cage a thrush and get it to sing, and he had one. By gow, it were a good 'un!

And then there were his dad and mother lived next door at yon side of a passage, and he used to work on the roads, sweep roads and that, and he were a little red-faced feller. I once talked to his son in hospital, and he said he were a good singer were his dad, old Jackson what lived there. He said he used to stand outside of a pub if he had nowt to get in with, and he'd cadge three ha'pence off somebody, so's he could get into t'pub. He called that a 'sneck lifter' and if he got into t'pub he knew he could get plenty of beer because he could sing. Somebody used to play t'piano, and he used to sing and his son lived there, Charlie, and they all lived till they were about eighty: they were long-living folks. Then there were an old woman lived in the next cottage that we used to call Auntie Min, Auntie Min Lightfoot, and she'd a brother Bill, he were Hoss Lightfoot's brother and he were a strong feller were Bill, but he were a bit queer. Then there were nobody lived in t'other house, what were called Potter's house. Some Varleys, basket makers, used to have it, and they used to come and pick fruit there but they got it altered, they had it done up, and they come and lived there out of Fostergate did Varleys, basketmakers.

Parsons

I once remember they had a concert at Sunday School, and they put me up on stage and I had to say a piece, and it were: "B is for . . .?" and they give me a bun and I had to say: "B is for Bernard eating a bun". I think it were Chambers what were t'parson then, Chambers. Then after him came a Mr Brookes; he were a good parson, and he had a family of five, three daughters and two sons. The oldest lad were called Philip, and t'youngest were called . . . now then . . . Gerald. I just forget what they called the girls. I can remember he used to take us at Sunday School, and I remember once I was doing summat wrong, turning round to kids in another class and laughing, and he didn't half give me a ringer across my ear. Well, we didn't go home and tell our mothers that he'd hitten us. If it had been today they'd have said don't go no more, but in our day we didn't dare go home and tell, because we should have gotten some more of the same!

He used to keep a goat or two for milking, and I know one night I were at t'station (I used to spend a lot of time at t'station with the porters) and when the twenty to eight train come in there were a goat on it, so t'station gaffer asks if I'll take goat to t'vicarage. So off I goes, and it were dark as pitch, no lights in t'streets then. I gets going down Back Lane and t'old goat slips t'band off, and off she goes! She were a dark coloured 'un and I couldn't see her. I hears some buckets rattling as I were going by where Iky lives, it were Sharlotte's then, and I hears these buckets rattling in t'coal house, so I goes to the house and I ask t'woman if she'll show me a light outside because this goat has gotten away from me. She comes with a candle and cops t'old goat and puts a band on it and I takes it to t'vicarage and they give me a tanner for taking it. He were a funny chap were Mr Brookes. When he were walking down the street, he always had a habit of turning his shoulder up.

I've heard 'em say that the living at Cawood for a parson were £350 a year. It wouldn't go far wouldn't £350 now! We used to go to church every Sunday night, me and Bill Hornshaw. Bill Mills used to go with us; he were up at Wetherell's the grocer's and he always used to come out with a pocket full of peas, right small, and a pea shooter. Anyway he lets fly at one of these lasses one night when she was sat in church, but by gow! she upped and she went for him. She says: "Don't think because I'm a girl I can't retaliate". I know at t'same time there were a little old butcher who lived where Ella Neville lives, they called him Tommy Grundill. By gow, he were a fat 'un! Fat were hung over his neck onto his collar, and he used to sit just three or four pews in front of us in church. One night Bill Mills gets his pea shooter out and he lets go and hits Tommy right at back of t'head. Well, he nearly jumped into t'pew in front of him, and he were that fat it used to take him five minutes to get turned round to see who had done it! He daren't say nowt, aye.

Mr Brookes he used to send 'em [his children] all away to boarding school and he used to have a maid. His wife Mrs Brookes, used to take us for choir practice. We used to have to go once a week. She'd come in front of us and she used to have a finger bent just like a claw. She would be making us do scales and she'd have her finger just in front on us, nearly scratching our noses. Bill Hornshaw used to go, he were t'biggest lad with us, well he used to have to blow the organ. He used to get tired of blowing did Bill, so he would let the wind out, he'd stop blowing and then t'old organ used to make a queer row and she would start on at him. One night he says: "I'm sick of listening to this row!" So she says: "Do you call my playing a row?"

He were at Cawood a lot of years were Mr Brookes, and then he went away to a place called Weaverthorpe, Helperthorpe I think it is. Mr Garbutt and Walt Elcock, they went and built a house there, they were building a schoolhouse for him. And Mac Lambert had to take him his bees, he had a little wagon, and he said oh by gow, wasn't he glad when he got them lot there!

Then after him a parson come called Mr Sykes. Now he were a big feller: he never had a wife but they said he'd had one and she'd been killed, but anyway, he were a right 'un for the lads was Mr Sykes. He used to have a cricket pitch in Stanley's field there in Rythergate; he used to have three men gardening and they spent hours at that cricket pitch for t'lads. He'd a swimming job for 'em, he got them a diving board and he used to take 'em in the river swimming. He had a physical culture class; he used to have a retired sergeant major come from York on an old motor bike for that. I were in it and I used to have some good do's, and he used to have boxing. He were a good 'un to us lads. He had a glee club, a glee class, and they won all the prizes there were around York. There used to be certificates that they'd won at it, all round the walls in the Old Boys' School.

He were a good man. And when he used to take us at church on a night, if he had owt to say, if he'd owt to square us up about, he used to walk out in front, he didn't go up into t'pulpit. We used to say: "Hey up, we're going to cop it tonight!", and if there were owt wrong he used to let you know about it.

Sometimes he would tell us he were 'spent up' and that we'd have to wait while he got some more money, but he were well off and he had a grand garden and a big goldfish pond; he'd some goldfish in there seven or eight inches long and he named 'em for t'lads he had in t'choir. He ran a good pack of scouts too, that's where Syd Elcock first got going [with scouting].

Me and Isy were t'last he married at Cawood and I know when I went to see him on the Saturday, he were just coming out of his house and he had two church wardens from t'place where he were going to, I think it were Aldborough or somewhere and he saw me coming and waved at us and shouted: "I'll be with you in a minute Bernard, I know what you want". Then he came to me, and he took all t'particulars, I never had no messing about

Bernard and Isy enjoying retirement in their new bungalow.

going so many times to see him and that. When he left Cawood they said he never came back again; but when he died he left a violin to Cawood, and they sold it for so much money. Well I think it was somewhere roundabout £500, and they had yon little statue put into the tower yonder, in memory of him.

Then the next parson we got, they called him Unthank, Mr Unthank. Now, he wasn't married and he used to ride about in a little Austin Seven, and he were a biggish feller. He allus used to remind me when he passed us, of old Mother Hubbard in her shoe! I know he used to go visiting when he first came and he went to an old woman, the boss's sister where I worked, and she were an old lass, she were getting on for eighty then. She says to the young woman who used to go and shop for her, she says: "I've seen the new parson, he's been to see me" and she says, "I'll tell you what Connie, he isn't one of nature's favourites". She meant he wasn't very good looking. But he were a very nice feller were Mr Unthank.

After Mr Unthank, I think it were Mr Crowe. He had a family, I think he'd two sets of twins and an odd 'un. And he were a nice feller, we never had a bad 'un. I don't know what folks is thinking about, saying that they don't go to church because they don't like t'parson. I think it's just an excuse. I think it's 'cos it's o'er much bother to get ready to go, and that's about what it is. Mr Crowe stopped for so many years, I think it'd be part of t'war-time, and then he went to Stillingfleet, and he died at Stillingfleet a few months ago.

After Mr Crowe we had Mr Shardlow, an oldish man, and he had a wife and I think he'd one daughter and two sons. She [the daughter] worked at the hospital at York for a long time I think. And then we had an old man used to come called Canon Lee, and by heck, that were a grand old feller. He come and fitted in for so long. He would come and he'd have his dinner with you; he'd stop and have his tea with you on a Sunday and he were a grand feller. I think a school at York is called after him, Canon Lee School. He was only just helping out while they got another parson. Then I think after Mr Shardlow retired we got Mr Bromley, and he'd a wife and two daughters had Mr Bromley and he stopped for seven or eight years and then we got Mr Capey and it's Mr Capey here now. Well, I never found fault with any of them, they've all been all right. [Rev Messer then Rev Stoker followed Rev Capey. The present vicar is Rev Ian Ellery.]

You know, it's a hard job running t'church today, there's many a time on a Sunday night there's only six in t'congregation, but we do very well with collections and with stewardship and that.